FINANCIAL REPORTING UNDER IAS/IFRS

VERA PALEA

FINANCIAL REPORTING UNDER IAS/IFRS

THEORETICAL BACKGROUND AND CAPITAL MARKET EVIDENCE – A EUROPEAN PERSPECTIVE

PETER LANG
Bern · Berlin · Bruxelles · Frankfurt am Main · New York · Oxford · Wien

Bibliographic information published by die Deutsche Nationalbibliothek
Die Deutsche Nationalbibliothek lists this publication in the Deutsche Nationalbibliografie; detailed bibliographic data is available on the Internet at ‹http://dnb.d-nb.de›.

British Library Cataloguing-in-Publication Data: A catalogue record for this book is available from The British Library, Great Britain

Library of Congress Cataloging-in-Publication Data

Palea, Vera.
Financial reporting under IAS/IFRS : theoretical background and capital market evidence–a European perspective / Vera Palea.
pages cm
Includes bibliographical references.
ISBN 978-3-03-431403-9
1. Financial statements–Standards–Europe. 2. Cash flow–Accounting–Standards.
3. Corporations–Valuation–Accounting–Standards. 4. Investment analysis–Europe.
5. Investments–Europe. I. Title.
HF5681.B2P148 2013
657'.302184–dc23

2013003591

ISBN 978-3-0343-1403-9 hb. ISBN 978-3-0351-0561-2 eBook

Hochfeldstrasse 32, CH-3012 Bern, Switzerland
info@peterlang.com, www.peterlang.com

Printed in Hungary

To Maurizio and Virginia

Foreword

Academic publications on accounting research are not always easily accessible for non-academics. This book is an exception and the first reason why I recommend it is read. It offers, in plain English, a comprehensive overview of the literature on the decision usefulness of financial statements, the issues around convergence of accounting standards, the IAS/IFRS adoption in the European Union, the effect of accounting disclosures on the cost of capital, and the ongoing fair value discussion.

Furthermore, the publication provides insight into the methodologies and approaches applied in accounting research, the difficulties encountered during such work, and the reasons to cautiously treat findings. It shows how easy it is to 'jump to conclusions' and ignore the objectives, scope and limitations of a particular piece of research. As often forgotten by practitioners, regulators, and even maybe standard setters, this may help increase the level of understanding among all stakeholders in the process of accounting standard setting. This is the second reason why I support the publication.

And finally, the themes discussed are quite topical. In particular, discussions about the decision usefulness of financial statements, describing and comparing the different qualitative characteristics of the IFRS Conceptual Framework, are of relevance, since the IASB will issue a discussion paper on the revision of this Framework later this year. The potential conflict between relevance, reliability, and understandability, and the role of stewardship are areas, among others, in which EFRAG has been and, will continue to be active in promoting the international debate. This publication adds to the available literature. Also, the overview of the findings on the benefits of revised accounting standards, measured by the cost of capital, the amount of (voluntary) disclosures and the level of analysts' attention provides important input to the standard setters in order to assess whether the expected benefits of new or amended accounting standards outweigh the estimated costs.

Overall, I consider this publication to be a valuable contribution to the ongoing national and international accounting standard-setting process.

Françoise Flores
EFRAG – European Financial Reporting Advisory Group
Chairman

Brussels, 30 January 2013

Table of Contents

Acknowledgments

I gratefully thank Françoise Flores, EFRAG Chairman, and Philippe Longerstaey, EFRAG Research Director, for their helpful and constructive comments on this book and their valuable advice.

I am also indebted to Laura Gambotti, Luisa Grimaldi and Sarah Nicol for their technical support.

Preface

The IAS/IFRS adoption all over Europe enforced by Regulation 1606/2002 represents one of the most important and controversial events in the history of accounting.

This research monograph deals with four key issues related to the IAS/IFRS adoption in Europe. It investigates whether the IAS/IFRS adoption improves financial reporting quality; whether it increases cross-country comparability of financial reporting; whether it lowers the cost of capital for firms; whether fair value accounting effectively contributes to improve financial reporting quality. Recently, the financial crisis has turned the spotlight on fair value accounting and led to a major policy debate on it. Understanding the contribution of IAS/IFRS to financial reporting quality and its usefulness to investors is therefore of great use to standard setters and policy makers.

This monograph organizes the research on the effects of the IAS/IFRS adoption in a systematic and comprehensive way so as to contribute to better understand the longstanding debate on the IAS/IFRS usefulness. It also provides the theoretical background within which the proposal of mandating IAS/IFRS in Europe has been developed. Defining the conceptual framework for the IAS/IFRS implementation is in fact a prerequisite for interpreting research results and for determining whether the European Regulator's goals have been achieved.

As is well known, the purpose of Regulation 1606/2002 is to improve financial reporting transparency, to increase cross-countries comparability and to promote an efficient capital market, that is, a reduction in the cost of capital for firms. This research monograph takes the Regulator's point of view and investigates whether, after the IAS/IFRS adoption, investors are provided with more useful information for their decision-making process and firms have access to a more efficient and cost-effective capital market. In this perspective, it provides updated evidence for evaluating the effects of the IAS/IFRS adoption in Europe and therefore represents a support for standard setting and policy making purposes.

In the end, this monograph shows that academic research is a valuable resource for standard setters and policy-makers. Financial reporting issues are often broad, difficult and complex. Academic research can however provide inputs to their resolution. It can help standard setters and regulators structure their thinking about such issues and provide evidence that inform the debate on them. From this point of view, this monograph shows how academic research can be successful in supporting the evaluation of possible effects of accounting standards and regulations.

Vera Palea

Chapter 1

The Decision Usefulness Approach to Financial Reporting and Capital Market Research

1. Introduction

Standard setters, regulators and policy makers all have a vital interest in the effect of financial reporting on the economy. This interest is due to the economic consequences associated with financial information. Financial information influences investors' behaviour with respect to portfolio selection, which affects security prices and, therefore, the terms on which a firm obtains additional financing. This, in turn, affects the firm's cost of capital and alters the nature of the projects undertaken.

In a capitalist economy, securities markets are the primary vehicle whereby capital is raised and allocated to competing investment needs. Consequently, it is socially desirable that these markets work well, that is, security prices provide correct values to guide the flow of investment funds. For example, a firm that has high-expected-value capital projects will be encouraged to invest in them if it receives a high price for its securities, and investment should be discouraged in firms that do not have high-expected-value capital projects. This will happen to the extent that security prices are close to fundamental value. Of course, this is what society would like, since investment capital is in scarce supply. Social welfare will be enhanced if scarce capital goes to the most productive alternatives.

However, security prices do not fully reflect fundamental value in the presence of inside information. Investors are aware of the estimation risk resulting from adverse selection and insider trading. Thus, a "lemons" phenomenon comes into play. Investors recognize that the market is not a "level playing field" and they either withdraw from the market or lower the amount they are willing to pay for any security. As a result, firms with high-quality investment projects will not receive a high price for their securities, and the market will not work as well as it should. A related problem arises if too many investors withdraw: the market becomes thin or, in other words, it loses depth, where depth is the number of shares that investors can buy or sell without affecting the market price. When depth is low, potential investors may not be able to buy or sell all they want of a security at the market price, which further hampers investment.

Empirical research has shown the importance of markets that work well for efficient capital allocation (Wurgler 2000). Countries with more firm-specific information incorporated into share prices enjoy in fact greater capital allocation efficiency. More firm-specific information incorporated into share prices is simply another way of saying that the market is working more effectively, or, equivalently, that there is less inside information.

Of course, developed capitalist economies have a variety of mechanisms for promoting the operation of securities markets. One such approach is accounting regulation. Just as a used car dealer who develops a reputation for honesty and fair dealing will enjoy higher sales prices, a firm with a credible policy of full disclosure will enjoy higher share prices and lower cost of capital. This is because full disclosure reduces investors' concerns about inside information.

2. Users of financial information

Financial information about firms is useful to many different players: investors, creditors, customers, suppliers, managers and other employees, regulators and government officials.

Investors, whether present or prospective, generally benefit from learning about how their investments have been and might be used by the managers of their companies.

One source of such information is the financial report that managers render to their boards of directors and shareholders. Financial reporting is the main formal means by which managers convey how they have managed firm resources over a period and the resultant financial condition of the firm at the end of that period. Prospective investors realize that once they have committed their funds to a firm by purchasing new shares directly or from an existing shareholder, they usually have little control over how the firm is managed. Non-controlling shareholders, in particular, have reason for concern. Consequently, they are usually interested in knowing how those over whom they have no control have used corporate resources.

Financial reporting also helps to motivate managers to operate their corporations in the interest of shareholders. Reporting in these areas is called the "stewardship" function of accounting. Stewardship, defined as accountability to present shareholders, is important for making decisions about providing resources to an entity. Information about stewardship is also important for voting on, or otherwise influencing, management's actions.

In addition to a report of stewardship, investors need data that help them determine the present and possible future economic value of their investments. If the firm's shares are actively traded in a market, shareholders can obtain unbiased estimates of the economic value of their investments from share prices. However, these prices are based, in part, on the information provided in financial reports. If this information is not relevant and reliable, its receipt does not change the value given to shares nor does it provide investors with the insights that they seek. Hence, prospective investors might have to incur costs to obtain information elsewhere or discount the amount they are willing to pay for the shares, using the information currently available to them. This makes shares worth less to them. As a result, present shareholders, including those who can exercise some control over the corporation, also benefit from their managers providing potential investors with financial reports which the investors find trustworthy.

Creditors are willing to know the likelihood that they will be repaid if they advance funds to the enterprise. They are also well advised to monitor how the funds are used, that the conditions imposed by loan covenants have been satisfied, and the extent to which the borrowers' ability to repay debt as promised has changed.

Suppliers to the corporation want to be paid for their goods and financial statements can provide useful information to this end. Customers who purchase products that require replacement or servicing must determine whether the vendor is likely to continue in business. Therefore, suppliers' and customers' interests are similar to those of creditors: they want assurance that their contractual relationships with the firm will be fulfilled as promised. Consequently, they tend to be concerned with the possibility that the firm will not be able to repay its debts or honour its obligations.

Because this ability is affected primarily by the firm's present and possible future losses rather than by increases in economic value, creditors and suppliers generally favour conservative accounting rules, or those where all expected losses are recorded and gains are delayed until they are almost certain.

Employees often find financial information useful for determining the extent to which their employer has prospered as well as the possibility that they might lose their jobs, or receive a promotion or pay raise. Managers' and other employees' bonuses as well as other benefits are often partially based on the financial performance of their firms, as measured by financial accounting data. Therefore, their concerns are similar to those of investors. They may also be compensated with share options that could become worthless (or considerably less valuable) if their firm's share prices drop. As a result, they are concerned with the impact of accounting figures on the share price performance in the market.

For these reasons, employees and managers tend to worry about the possibility that their firm has performed badly, resulting in a loss of their positions, investments in the firm's shares and retirement plans.

Furthermore, those managers whose bonuses, job security, and prospects are based on financial accounting data, rather than on share prices, have reason to want financial reports to present numbers that benefit them. For example, they would like the statements to show that they have done at least as well as predicted by share analysts and therefore report net earnings that are sufficient for them to earn bonuses.

Tax authorities in many countries also base tax liabilities on financial statement data. Consequently, these authorities are concerned about the validity of the numbers presented in financial statements. Antitrust authorities generally make their decisions on market performance analyses based on rates of return and market shares constructed from data presented in financial reports. Regulatory authorities, such as the Stock Exchange Commission (SEC) in the United States and the European Securities and Markets Authority (ESMA), are charged with assuring investors that stock markets are "fair" and that the financial reports they receive are unbiased and, if possible, include information that is useful for them or their agents to assist in determining the value and performance of publicly traded equity and debt investments. Public policy towards firms, especially industry regulation, is often based on the profits or losses reported in financial statements. Governments and their agencies have a wide range of interests in the reporting of an enterprise's activities: for instance, accounts also serve as the basis for national income and similar statistics. The general public is affected by firms in a wide variety of ways, and accounting statements may help provide relevant information.

Although different users of financial statements require different information for very different reasons, they do however have one interest in common: they want numbers that they can trust.

3. The usefulness approach to financial reporting

Both the International Accounting Standard Board (IASB) and Financial Accounting Standard Board (FASB) recognize the existence of diverse and pluralistic user groups. However, they focus on what they call primary user groups, i.e. investors and creditors, who are assumed to be mainly interested in the amounts, timing, and uncertainties of the firm's future cash flows. (IASB 2010)

Existing and potential investors, lenders and other creditors have in fact the most critical and immediate need for the information in financial reports and many cannot require the entity to provide the information to them directly.

According to both the IASB and FASB, the main objective of financial reporting is to provide information that is useful to present and potential investors, lenders and other creditors in making decisions about providing resources to the entity (IASB 2010).

The term "investors" refers to present and potential equity holders and their advisers, and the term "creditors" refers to present and potential lenders and their advisers.

Investors include both individual and institutional shareholders and the firm's board of directors, who act on behalf of shareholders. Although they are not strictly investors *per se*, equity analysts make extensive use of financial statements and are an integral part of the investing process.

Creditors are present and potential lenders who need financial information about their customers to determine the terms of credit. In a broader sense, creditors also include tax authorities and other individuals or entities that have claims on the firm ahead of shareholders.

The terms investors and creditors may therefore comprehend security analysts and advisors, brokers, lawyers, regulatory agencies, and others who advise or represent the interests of investors and creditors or who are otherwise interested in how investors and creditors are faring.

As mentioned, existing and potential shareholders need information to estimate the value of the firm's shares and make wealth-enhancing capital-allocation decisions, which are also beneficial to the economy. The board of directors has the responsibility for implementing strategies and policies that create wealth and ensure that management acts in the interests of the shareholders. In this role, the board needs to be able to evaluate and reward management's efforts, abilities, and decisions, particularly management's capital-allocation decisions.

Getting paid is certainly a major concern of the holders of interest-bearing debt, but their concern goes beyond this. While loans from commercial banks typically have maturities of a few years, corporate bonds have much longer maturities. The bonds may be sold before they mature, and changes in the value of the firm affect the market value of those bonds. Bondholders are therefore concerned with the value of the entire firm.

The resource allocation decisions of these users include determining whether to buy, sell, or hold securities and whether to lend funds or call existing debt issued by the entity.

Therefore, many individuals and entities have a vested interest in understanding the financial well-being of a firm. When the firm works well, securities pricing is correct, the allocation of capital in the economy is efficient and everyone is better off.

Decisions by existing and potential investors about buying, selling or holding equity and debt instruments depend on the returns that they expect from an investment in those instruments, for example dividends, principal and interest payments or market price increases. Similarly, decisions by existing and potential lenders and other creditors about providing or setting loans and other forms of credit depend on the principal and interest payments or other returns that they expect.

Investors', lenders' and other creditors' expectations about returns depend on their assessment of the amount, timing and uncertainty of future net cash inflows to the firm. Consequently, existing and potential investors, lenders and other creditors need information to help them assess the prospects for the future net cash inflows of a firm. However, financial reports are not designed to show the value of a firm, but to provide information to help existing and potential investors, lenders and other creditors to estimate the value of the firm. Even though investors and creditors are the primary users of financial information, financial reports do not and cannot provide all the information that existing and potential investors, lenders and other creditors need. Obviously, these users also need to consider pertinent information from other sources, for example, general economic conditions and expectations, political events and political climate, and industry and company outlooks.

4. The qualitative characteristics of accounting information

The qualitative characteristics of accounting information are the attributes that make the information provided in financial statements useful to users.

In order to be useful, financial information should possess two fundamental qualitative characteristics: relevance and faithful representation (IASB 2010).

There are also some enhancing qualitative characteristics, which are complementary to the fundamental characteristics: comparability, verifiability, timeliness and understandability. Enhancing qualitative characteristics distinguish more useful information from less useful information. They enhance the decision-usefulness of financial reporting information that is relevant and faithfully represented.

Information is relevant when it is capable of making a difference to a financial statement user's decisions. Relevant information has predictive value, i. e. it helps users to evaluate the potential effects of past, present, or future transactions or other events on future cash flows, and confirmatory value, i. e. it helps to confirm or correct their previous evaluations. Making the information available to users before it loses its capacity to influence their decisions, i.e. timeliness, is another aspect of relevance. Information should be available to decision makers before it loses its capacity to influence decisions. Having relevant information available at an early stage can enhance its capacity to influence decisions and a lack of timeliness can rob information of its potential usefulness.

An entity-specific aspect of relevance is materiality. Information is material if its omission or misstatement could influence the resource allocation decisions that users make on the basis of financial information about a specific reporting entity. In other words, materiality is an entity-specific aspect of relevance based on the nature, or magnitude, or both, of the items to which information relates in the context of an individual entity's financial report.

Faithful representation means that the information reflects the real-world economic phenomena that it purports to represent. Real-world economic phenomena are economic resources and obligations and the transactions or other events that change them.

To be a perfectly faithful representation, a depiction must be complete, neutral and free from error.

A complete depiction includes all information necessary for users to understand the phenomenon being depicted.

A neutral depiction is without bias in the selection or presentation of financial information. A neutral depiction is not slanted, weighted, emphasised, de-emphasised or otherwise manipulated to increase the probability that financial information will be received more favourably or unfavourably by users. Neutral information does not mean information with no purpose or no influence on behaviour. On the contrary, relevant financial information is, by definition, capable of making a difference in users' decisions.

Free of errors means that there are no errors or omissions in the description of the phenomenon, and the process used to produce the reported information has been selected and applied with no errors in the process.

As mentioned, comparability, verifiability, timeliness and understandability are qualitative characteristics that enhance the usefulness of information that is relevant and faithfully represented.

Comparability, which includes consistency, is the quality of information that enables users to identify similarities in and differences between two sets of economic phenomena. As a consequence, it is undesirable if similar transactions, events, or conditions look different or if different transactions, events, or conditions look alike. Consistency helps achieve comparability because it refers to the use of the same accounting policies, either from period to period within an entity or in a single period across entities.

Verifiability means that different knowledgeable and independent observers could reach consensus, although not necessarily complete agreement, that a particular depiction is a faithful representation. Quantified information need not to be a single point estimate to be verifiable. A range of possible amounts and the related probabilities can also be verified.

Timeliness means having information available to decision-makers in time to be considered in their decisions. Finally, understandability is the quality of information that enables users who have reasonable knowledge of business and economic activities and financial reporting, and who study the information with reasonable diligence, to comprehend its meaning. However, when underlying economic phenomena are particularly complex, fewer users may understand the financial information depicting those phenomena. In these cases, some users may need to seek the aid of an adviser. Information that is relevant and faithfully represented should not be excluded from financial reports solely because it may be too complex or too difficult for some users to understand without assistance.

Qualitative characteristics are subject to the cost constraint. Reporting financial information imposes costs, and it is important that those costs are justified by the benefits of reporting that information. Costs include direct and indirect costs incurred by both preparers and users of financial information, as well as by auditors and regulators. Assessing whether the benefits exceed the costs is inherently subjective because it is not possible to obtain qualitative data on all costs and benefits. However, the requirement to assess benefits and costs means that standard setters need to consider practicality as well as concept.

5. Capital market research and standard setting issues

As already mentioned, the decision usefulness approach to financial reporting underlies the conceptual framework of both the IASB and FASB. According to them, the main objective of financial reporting is to provide information that is useful to investors, creditors and others in making investment, credit and similar resource allocation decisions. Moreover, the IASB states that IASB and FASB's responsibilities require them to focus on the needs of participants in capital markets (IASB 2010 BC 1.16).

The extent to which research can inform standard setting has been the subject of debate among academics for many years. As one of the major uses of accounting data by capital market participants relates to valuation, accounting research has long been focusing on the relation between accounting amounts and share prices or returns. Capital market research has therefore been used as a basis for choosing the best accounting policies and evaluating the economic consequences of alternative accounting policies on security prices. Accounting policies that most affect security prices have been considered to be the most useful and with the highest information content.

The research stream which compares different accounting policies for standard setting purposes by examining their association with securities prices is also called "value relevance" research (Holthausen and Watts, 2001). In the last decades, value relevance research has been the prevalent way to address accounting standard-setting issues.

Value relevance studies use various valuation models to structure their tests, and typically use equity market value as the valuation benchmark to assess how well particular accounting amounts reflect information used by investors.

As outlined by Barth *et al.* (2001), in the accounting literature an accounting number is defined as value relevant if it has a predicted association with equity market values.

The primary purpose for conducting tests of value relevance is to extend the knowledge regarding the relevance and reliability of accounting amounts as reflected in equity values. Equity values reflect an accounting amount if the two are correlated.

Relevance and reliability are the two primary criteria that standard setters use for choosing among accounting alternatives. As mentioned, an accounting amount is relevant if it is capable of making a difference to financial statement users' decisions, whereas an accounting number is reliable if it represents what it purports to represent.

Value relevance as defined in the academic literature is therefore a way to operationalize the criteria of relevance and reliability (i. e. faithful representation). In fact, an accounting amount will be value relevant, i. e. it will have a predicted significant relation with share prices, only if the amount reflects information relevant to investors in valuing a firm and is measured reliably enough to be reflected in share prices. Only if an accounting amount is relevant to a financial statement user, can it make a difference to that user's decisions.

Value relevance tests are joint tests of relevance and reliability. In fact, although finding value relevance indicates the accounting amount is relevant and reliable, at least to some degree, it is difficult to attribute the cause of lack of value relevance to one or the other attribute.

Value relevance research is not the only type of research potentially relevant to standard setters. In fact, there are a variety of ways researchers can operationalize relevance and reliability, or the secondary dimensions of these primary criteria that standard setters consider when making standard setting decisions. Thus, a variety of research approaches can yield insight into standard-setting issues. However, in large part because of the development of the notion of market efficiency, capital market research in finance and accounting has been prevalent.

Value relevance studies rely on the hypothesis that markets are efficient with respect to financial information. Market efficiency is a central feature of capital market research and deals with how capital markets process information in general, and financial reporting information specifically.

Fama (1970) states that a securities market is efficient if security prices "fully" reflect all the information available. The market is efficient with respect to some specified information system if, and only if, security prices behave as if everyone observes the information system.

Fama also delineates three major forms of market efficiency: weak, semi-strong and strong. The market is efficient in the weak form if prices fully reflect information regarding the past sequence of prices. This form of market efficiency has obvious implications for technical analysis and it includes the random walk theory of stock prices. The market is efficient in the semi-strong form if prices fully reflect all publicly available information, including financial statement data. Trading strategies based on published financial statement data will not lead to abnormal returns. The market is efficient in the strong form if prices fully reflect all information, including inside information. Hence, even having access to private information will not lead to strategies promising abnormal expected returns.

The implication of assuming that market efficiency exists is particularly important for standard-setting. In fact, market efficiency in the semi-strong form provides the best climate for mandating disclosure. Motivation for requiring disclosure is essential to bring private information into public domain. In a market that is not efficient in a strong form, this is a potentially substantive issue, as privately held information is not reflected in prices. Once data are placed in the public domain, semi-strong form market efficiency provides the assurance that such data will be fully reflected in prices. Thus, requiring public disclosure is an effective remedy (at least in terms of securities price) for any perceived undesirable effects associated with the presence of non-publicly available data.

However, as outlined by Scott (2009), improved financial reporting also has a key role under the hypothesis of market inefficiency. In fact, according to anomalies studies (Lee 2001 for a review), when share prices are mispriced relative to the prices they would have if markets were fully efficient, rational investors discover such mispricing over time and take advantage of it, driving prices towards fundamental values.

To the extent that securities markets are not fully efficient, this can only increase the importance of financial reporting. Overall, improved financial reporting, by giving investors more help in predicting efficient firm value, speeds up share price response to the full information content of financial statements. By reducing the costs of rational analysis, better reporting may reduce the extent of investors' behavioural biases. Financial reporting therefore reduces inefficiencies by making the mispricing area between inefficient market price of firms and efficient market price as small as possible.

It must also be said that value relevance research for standard setting has been criticized by some researchers because it focuses only on equity investors, who are not the only users of financial statements (e. g. Holthausen and Watts 2001). With a variety of demand for financial reporting from parties other than stock market investors, value relevance tests may be less relevant to the goal of standard setters and the objectives of financial reporting. This conclusion reflects the fact that accounting standards are essentially a public good and, thus, standard setters develop standards after making social welfare trade-off.

The IASB and FASB themselves however underline that responsibility requires them to focus on the needs of participants in capital markets (IASB 2010 BC1.16). Existing and potential investors, lenders and other creditors have the most critical and immediate need for the information in financial reports and many cannot require the entity to provide the information for them directly.

Furthermore, since investors are providers of risk capital to firms, the provision of financial statements that meet their needs also meet most of the needs of other users that financial statements can satisfy. As a result, investors' needs can be considered as highly representative of the needs of a wide range of users.

The IASB also argues that information that meets the needs of the specified primary users is likely to meet both the needs of users in jurisdictions with a corporate governance model defined in the context of shareholders and those with a corporate governance model defined in the context of all types of stakeholders (IASB BC 1.16).

Of course, other uses of financial statements exist beyond equity investment as, for instance, management compensation and debt contracting.

Thus, research relating directly to management compensation and debt contracting can also inform standard setting (Watts and Zimmerman 1986). However, as many researchers have highlighted (e.g. Barth *et al.* 2001), financial statements are not intended to apply directly to management compensation contracts. More importantly, the possible contracting uses of financial statements in no way diminish the importance of value relevance research and it cannot be construed as a criticism of this kind of research.

This research monograph is on capital market research on changes in accounting standards. It focuses on the IAS/IFRS adoption in Europe, which is one of the most important and controversial events in the history of accounting. This monograph analyses both accounting theory and empirical research related to such an event by considering accounting literature published in leading accounting journals and selected working papers starting from the 1990s.

The monograph is organized as follows. In chapter 2, the history of the converging process in financial reporting before the IAS/IFRS mandatory adoption is traced and a literary review on early evidence about the effects of changes in accounting standard sets is provided.

As international trade accelerated and capital markets became globalized, the investment community and the accounting profession started calling for financial reports which could be easily understood and compared irrespective of the country of origin of the company concerned. Given the increasing integration of capital markets and the resulting debate over the most appropriate measurement techniques, evidence on the relative informativeness of different accounting standard sets have been considered of great importance to standard setters. As a result, capital market research has long been focused on a comparison among different accounting standard sets in order to assess their relative informativeness and rank them according to their usefulness to investors.

Chapter 3 outlines the theoretical background in which the proposal of adopting the IAS/IFRS was developed and taken by the European Regulator. Defining the conceptual framework for Regulation 1606/2002 is a prerequisite for determining whether the Regulator's goals have been achieved. Chapter 3 also examines the capital market effects of adopting IAS/IFRS from the investors' point of view. As a result, the decision-usefulness of financial reporting under IAS/IFRS is investigated.

Chapter 4, instead, examines the effects of adopting IAS/IFRS from a firm's point of view. The effects of adopting IAS/IFRS on the firm's cost of capital are therefore discussed.

Finally, chapter 5 investigates the contribution of fair value accounting to financial reporting quality and its usefulness to investors. Fair value accounting represents the main difference between IAS/IFRS and the Fourth and Seventh Directives in Europe, which are based on historical cost accounting. Assessing the relevance and reliability of fair value estimates therefore provides useful insight into the role that fair value accounting plays in increasing financial reporting quality.

All these issues are of considerable interest and importance especially for standard setting purposes and policy making, whose primary aims are to provide investors with useful information for their decision-making process and to allow firms to have access to a more efficient and cost-effective capital market.

References

Ball, R., and P. Brown (1968), "An empirical evaluation of accounting income numbers", *Journal of Accounting research*, 6, 159–178.

Ball, R. (2006), "IFRS: Pros and cons for investors", *Accounting and Business Research*, International Accounting Policy Forum, 5–27.

Barth, M.E., G. Clinch and T. Shibano (1999), "International accounting harmonization and global equity markets", *Journal of Accounting and Economics*, 26, 201–235.

Barth, M.E., W.H. Beaver and W.R. Landsman (2001), "The relevance of the value relevance literature for financial accounting standard setting: another view", *Journal of Accounting and Economics*, 31, 77–104.

Barth, M.E. (2007), "Standard-setting measurement issues and the relevance of research", *Accounting and Business Research*, Special Issue: International Accounting Policy Forum, 7–15.

Benston, G.J., M. Bromwich, R.E. Litan and A. Wagenhofer (2006), *Worlwide financial reporting. The development and future of accounting standards*, Oxford, Oxford University Press.

Biondi, Y. and T. Suzuki (2007), "Socio-economic impact of international accounting standards: an international socio-economic review", *Socio-Economic Review*, 5.

Bush T. (2005), *'Divided by common language'. Where economics meets the law: US versus non-US financial reporting models*, ICAEW, June.

Carnegie, G. D. and C. J. Napier (2002), "Exploring comparative international accounting history", *Accounting, Auditing & Accountability Journal*, 15(5).

Choi, F. D. S. and R. M. Levich (1990), *The capital market effects of international accounting diversity*, Dow Jones-Irwin, Homewood.

Choi, F. D. S. and R. M. Levich (1996), "Accounting diversity", in B. Stell (ed.), *The European equity markets*, Royal Institute of International Affairs, London.

Ciesielski, J. (2008), "It's not a small world, after all: the SEC goes international", *The Analyst's Accounting Observer*, 16(11), July.

Cooper, S. (2007), "Discussion of 'Standard-setting measurement issues and the relevance of research'", *Accounting and Business Research*, Special Issue: International Accounting Policy Forum, 17–18.

Deloitte (2008), *2008 IFRS survey. Where are we today?*

Esty, D. C. and D. Geradin (eds.) (2001), *Regulatory competition and economic integration*, Oxford, Oxford University Press.

Evans, L. (2004), "Language, translation and the problem of international accounting communication", *Accounting, Auditing & Accountability Journal*, 17(2).

Fama, E. F. (1970), "Efficient capital markets: a review of theory and empirical work", *Journal of Finance*, XXV, 383–417.

Global Accounting Alliance (2008), *Getting to the heart of the issue: can financial reporting be made simpler and more useful?*, December.

Gray, S. J., G. K. Meek and C. B. Roberts (1994), "Financial deregulation, stock exchange listing choice, and the development of a European capital market", in Zimmerman, V. K. (ed.), *The new Europe: recent political and economic implications for accountants and accounting*, Center for International Education and Research in Accounting, University of Illinois.

Holthausen, R. W. and R. L. Watts (2001), "The relevance of the value-relevance literature for financial accounting standard setting", *Journal of Accounting and Economics*, 31, 3–75.

ICAEW (Institute of Charted Accountants in England and Wales) (2007), *EU implementation of IFRS and the fair value directive. A report for the European Commission*, October.

Kothari, S. P. (2001), "Capital markets research in accounting", *Journal of Accounting and Economics,* 31, 105–231.

Kothari, J. and E. Barone (2011), *Advanced financial accounting. An international approach*, Prentice Hall – Financial Times.

Lee, C. M. C. (2001), "Market efficiency and accounting research: a discussion of 'Capital market research in accounting' by S. P. Kothari", *Journal of Accounting and Economics*, September, 233–253.

Lennard, A. (2007), "Stewardship and the objectives of financial statements: a comment on IASB's preliminary views on an improved conceptual framework for financial reporting: the objective of financial reporting and qualitative characteristics of decision-useful financial reporting information", *Accounting in Europe*, 4(1), 51–66.

Lev, B. (1974), "On the association between operating leverage and risk", *Journal of Financial and Quantitative Analysis*, September, 627–640.

Lev, B. (1989), "On the usefulness of earnings and earnings research: lessons and directions from two decades of empirical research", *Journal of Accounting Research*, 27, supplement, 153–192.

Lev, B. and S.R. Thiagarajan (1993), "Fundamental information analysis", *Journal of Accounting Research*, Autumn, 190–215.

Maddison, A. (2001), *The world economy. A millennial perspective*, OECD, Paris.

Michie, R. (2008), *The global securities market. A history*, Oxford, Oxford University Press.

Nobes, C. and R.B. Parker (2010), *Comparative International Accounting*, 11th edn. Financial Times Press.

Parker, R.H. (1983), "Some international aspects of accounting", in S.J. Gray (ed.), *International accounting and transnational decision*, Butterworths, London.

PricewaterhouseCoopers (2006), *IFRS. The investors' view*, February, <http://download.pwc.com/ie/pubs/ifrs_survey.pdf>, accessed January, 2013.

Scott, W.R. (2009), *Financial Accounting Theory*, 5th edn., Prentice-Hall.

Watts, R.L. and J.L. Zimmermann (1986), *Positive Accounting Theory*, London, Prentice-Hall.

Wheatley, S. (1988), "Some tests of international equity integration", *Journal of Financial Economics*, 21(2).

Wurgler, J. (2000), "Financial markets and the allocation of capital", *Journal of Financial Economics*, 58, 187–214.

Chapter 2

The Converging Process in Financial Reporting

1. Introduction

A notable feature of the world economy since the Second World War has been the globalization of economic activity. This has led to the spreading round the world not just of goods and services but also of people, technologies and concepts.

From the point of view of financial reporting, the two most important aspects of globalization are international trade and foreign direct investments. At the regional level, economic integration and freer trade have been encouraged through the European Union and through institutions such as the North American Free Trade Area (NAFTA). The liberalization has also been due to the dismantling of trade barriers under the General Agreement on Tariffs and Trade (GATT) and its successor the World Trade Organization (WTO).

Moreover, most national currencies in the European Union, with the notable exception of the pound sterling, were replaced in 1999 by a single currency, the euro.

At the same time as international trade and foreign direct investments grew, capital markets became increasingly globalized, as well. This was made possible by the deregulation of the leading national financial markets, the speed of financial innovation, the dramatic advances in the electronic technology of communications and growing links between domestic and world financial markets.

As international trade speeded up and capital markets became globalized, the investment community and the accounting profession started calling for financial reports which could be easily understood and compared irrespective of the country of origin of the company concerned. As a result, academic research started focusing on a comparison of different accounting standard sets in order to identify the most accurate, useful and desirable one.

2. Convergence in accounting standards

Nowadays, investors seek investment opportunities all over the world in the same way as companies seek capital at the lowest price anywhere. Cross-border mergers and investment transactions have dramatically increased, as well.

The investment community and the accounting profession have therefore become quickly aware of the need to develop international accounting standards and of the benefits of a common global accounting language. National accounting standards made sense when companies raised money and investors and lenders looked for investment opportunities in their home country.

As a result, investors, managers and all the standard setting constituents have started calling for the development of a global set of comprehensive high-quality accounting standards which could make it easier to compare investment options and reduce costs for issuers by no longer requiring them to prepare financial statements under more than one standard. A common financial language, if applied consistently, could in fact help investors compare the financial results of companies operating in different jurisdictions and provide greater opportunity for investment. The removal of differences in national accounting standards should also reduce information asymmetries as well as the cost of capital and open new opportunities for diversification and improved investment returns.

Despite different historical and cultural backgrounds that have led to differences in national accounting standards, today there is an overwhelming need for accounting principles to be harmonised worldwide.

As highlighted by Ball (2006), a single set of high quality global accounting standards would provide different advantages.

First of all, it would provide more accurate comprehensive and timely information, which should in turn lead to more informed valuation in the equity markets and, hence, to a lower risk for investors. It would also provide easier access to foreign capital markets. Reduction of differences in accounting standards internationally assists to some degree in removing barriers to cross-border acquisitions and divestitures, which should reward investors with higher takeover premiums.

A single set of high quality global accounting standards is also expected to lower the cost of capital for companies both in absolute terms and in comparison with other firms. By eliminating discrepancies in financial reporting due to differences in national accounting standards, it should level the playing field for firms worldwide and make the capital markets more efficient. Global standards would not require reconciliation to the accounting standards of other countries, thus improving comparability of financial data across borders. By eliminating many international differences in accounting standards, a single set of global accounting standards would eliminate many of the adjustments analysts historically make in order to make companies' financial statements comparable internationally. Reducing the cost of processing financial information should also increase the efficiency with which the stock market incorporates it in prices.

Beside a greater transparency and a greater understandability due to a common financial language, other advantages related to global standards would be reduced national standard-setting costs; easier regulation of securities markets; uniform training for international audit firms and, therefore, better quality of their work on a global basis; portability of knowledge and education across national boundaries.

One step towards a single set of global accounting standards is represented by the adoption of the international accounting standards IAS/IFRS[1] by many countries worldwide. With Regulation 1606/2002, from 2005 onwards listed companies in the European Union were required to publish their consolidated financial statements using IAS/IFRS rather than national generally accepted accounting principles (GAAP). IAS/IFRS or local variants have also been adopted in countries as diverse as Australia, Canada,

1 IAS were issued by the International Accounting Standard Committee (IASC), predecessor of the International Accounting Standard Board (IASB) till 2000. IFRS are issued by the IASB.

Hong Kong, Central and Eastern Europe, including Russia, parts of the Middle East and Africa. The next wave of transitioning territories include India, Japan, China and much of South America. These territories are likely to adopt IAS/IFRS, at least for part of their economies, in the near future. The details vary, but the trend towards global standards is clear and strong. Several other countries have not yet adopted IAS/IFRS, but have established convergence projects that are most likely to lead to their acceptance of IAS/IFRS, in one form or another in the not too distant future. The appendix reports the current use of IAS/IFRS in the countries of G20.

In 2007, for instance, the Securities and Exchange Commission (SEC) in the United States of America announced two important initiatives. The first initiative has been the rule that eliminated reconciliations from IAS/IFRS to US GAAP required to be given by foreign private companies listed on US markets. Reconciliations are a cost and burden to companies and yet the general view is that hardly any use was made of them by investors. The second initiative has been the announcement that IAS/IFRS would be permitted in the US markets as an alternative to US GAAP, although the timescale is in this case lengthy and subject to various conditions.

All these initiatives are very important as they underpin a movement towards IAS/IFRS as a single set of globally accepted accounting standards.

3. Value relevance studies on different accounting standard sets: A theoretical background

Given the increasing integration of capital markets and the resulting debate over the most appropriate measurement techniques, evidence on the relative informativeness of different accounting standard sets has been considered of great importance to standard setters.

Empirical research has long been focusing on the comparison among different accounting standard sets in order to assess their relative informativeness and rank them according to their usefulness to investors. The leitmotif in this research area has been the investors' reaction to differences in accounting techniques.

As one of the major uses of accounting data relates to valuation, accounting research has focused mostly on the relation between accounting amounts and share prices or returns. As a result, capital market research has been used for decades as a basis for choosing the best accounting policies and evaluating the economic consequences of alternative accounting policies on security prices. Accounting policies that most affect security prices have been considered to be the most useful and to have the most information content.

The research stream which compares different accounting policies for standard setting purposes by examining their association with securities prices is called "value relevance" research (Holthausen and Watts, 2001).

As outlined by Barth *et al.* (2001), in the accounting literature an accounting number is defined as value relevant if it has a predicted association with equity market values.

The primary purpose for conducting tests of value relevance is to extend knowledge regarding the relevance and reliability (i.e. faithful representation) of accounting amounts as reflected in equity values. Equity values reflect an accounting amount if the two are correlated. As discussed in chapter 1, relevance and reliability are the two primary criteria the standard setters use for choosing among accounting alternatives. An accounting amount is relevant if it is capable of making a difference to financial statement users' decisions, whereas an accounting number is reliable if it represents what it purports to represent.

Value relevance as defined in the academic literature is a way to operationalize the criteria of relevance and reliability. An accounting amount will be value relevant, that is, with a predicted significant relation with share prices, only if the amount reflects information relevant to investors in valuing a firm and is measured reliably enough to be reflected in share prices. Only if an accounting amount is relevant to a financial statement user, it is capable of making a difference to that user's decisions.

Value relevance tests are joint tests of relevance and reliability. In fact, although finding value relevance indicates the accounting amount is relevant and reliable, at least to some degree, it is difficult to attribute the lack of value relevance either to one or the other.

Value relevance studies use various valuation models to structure their tests, and they typically use equity market value as the valuation benchmark to assess how well particular accounting amounts reflect the information used by investors. Value relevance studies determine whether an accounting number is useful for valuing the firm by investigating if the accounting number is associated with stock prices.

According to Holthausen and Watts (2001), value relevance studies can be classified into three categories as follows. The "relative association" studies compare the association between stock market values (or changes in values) and alternative bottom line numbers. Some studies, for instance, examine whether the association of an earnings number, calculated under a proposed standard, is more highly associated with stock market values or returns (over long windows) than earnings calculated under the existing standard. Other studies compare the associations of foreign GAAP and domestic GAAP earnings with stock market values or returns (over long windows).

These studies usually test for differences in the R^2 of regressions using different bottom line accounting numbers. The accounting number with the greater R^2 is described as more value relevant.

The "incremental association" studies test the usefulness of individual financial statement components or disclosure. They usually use regressions to investigate whether the accounting number of interest is helpful in explaining value or returns (over long windows) given other specified variables. That accounting number is typically deemed to be value relevant if its estimated regression coefficient is significantly different from zero.

Finally, the "marginal information content" studies investigate whether a particular accounting number adds to the information set available to investors. They typically use event studies (short window return studies) to determine if the release of an accounting number (conditional on other information released) is associated with value changes. In this case, price reactions are considered to be evidence of value relevance.

Value relevance studies rely basically on two different theories in order to draw inferences: the "direct valuation" theory and the "inputs-to equity-valuation" theory.

In the "direct valuation" theory, accounting earnings are intended to either measure, or be highly associated with, equity market value changes or levels (via permanent income). The book value of equity under this theory is intended to either measure, or be highly associated with, equity market values. Given direct valuation theory, standard setters would be interested in the results of a study of the relative stock price associations of alternative accounting earnings or book value of equity measures.

In the "inputs-to-equity valuation" theory, instead, the role of accounting is to provide information on inputs to valuation models that investors use in valuing firms' equity. Under an "inputs-to-equity valuation" theory, the focus is on how investors use an accounting number in their valuation models. As a result, that inference requires a valuation model and an assumed link between the accounting number and a variable entering into the valuation model. Value relevance studies relying on an inputs-to-equity valuation theory generally perform an incremental association study.

In this chapter, the history of the converging process in financial reporting before the IAS/IFRS mandatory adoption is traced and a literary review on early evidence about the effects of changes in accounting standard sets is provided. As mentioned above, the focus is on accounting literature published in leading accounting journals and selected working papers starting from the 1990s.

4. The relative informativeness of different accounting standard sets: The case of reconciliation Form 20-F

The discussion on the relative informativeness of different accounting standard sets was opened up by a discussion in the United States over the appropriate listing requirements for foreign stocks and aimed at verifying the usefulness of Form 20-F required to non-US firms listed on the US stock market. In fact, non-US firms could list their securities in the United States either by issuing a prospectus and satisfying a panoply of SEC reporting requirements, or by listing registered American Depository Receipts (ADRs) and filing an annual Form 20-F and a semi-annual Form 6-K which reconciled earnings based on foreign generally accepted accounting principles (GAAP) with the corresponding US GAAP numbers. Although these requirements were less extensive than those for US firms, the American Stock

Exchange (AMEX) and the New York Stock Exchange (NYSE) started lobbying the US congress and the US Securities and Exchange Commission (SEC) to ease these requirements further. The AMEX and NYSE concern was that the SEC requirements placed them at a competitive disadvantage in listing foreign firms since many other countries' Regulators allowed mutual recognition without restatements.

As a result, the lobbying activities by the AMEX and NYSE triggered a debate in the United States about global competition for exchange listing. In this debate, the SEC criticized the quality of the financial reporting requirements in most other countries throughout the world. SEC's concern about non-US accounting standards focused on the vulnerability of reported earnings to earnings management, as well as the potential lack of informativeness and timeliness of reported accounting numbers – primarily accounting income –, undue reliance on tax regulations for financial reporting measurement rules and the infrequency and the paucity of disclosure.

Amir, Harris and Venuti (1993) has been the first study on the value relevance of the reconciliation form 20-F. They examine Form 20-F, which includes a reconciliation of earnings and book value to US GAAP from home-country accounting principles, to address two questions. Firstly, whether differences in US and non-US GAAP, as summarized in the aggregate reconciliations of earnings and book value, are value relevant. That is, whether the reconciliation of accounting data to US GAAP increase the associations between accounting measures and price. Secondly, what differences in accounting practices, still reflected in the components of the reconciliation, are specifically value relevant. The idea is that if reconciliation data do not result to be value relevant, then it would be harder to argue that such data were necessary. Amir, Harris and Venuti use regressions of returns and market-to-book ratios over earnings reported under non-US GAAP and reconciliation data. Their results suggest that reconciliations of earnings and shareholders' equity to US GAAP are value relevant, consistently with US GAAP being more value relevant than non-US-GAAP, and this result holds both in aggregate and for some specific components, in particular property revaluations and capitalized goodwill.

Rees and Elgers (1997) use the same methodology as in Amir, Harris and Venuti, but analyze the value relevance of income and shareholders' equity reconciliations in periods prior to their disclosure. Their aim is to test whether the reconciliation form is itself the source of the information or whether some of the value relevant information in the SEC-mandated disclosures is available to the market from other sources. As supposed, they find that the SEC-mandated disclosures are not the exclusive source of value relevant information, thus calling into question the necessity of Form 20-F.

Harris and Muller (1999) use Form 20-F in order to evaluate the relative informativeness of IAS and US GAAP, specifically. The Form 20-F permits them to directly relate the firm value with both IAS and US GAAP accounting measures as implemented by foreign firms listed in the US. Such firms prepared in fact their home country financial statements using IAS and then reconciled from IAS to US GAAP in their Form 20-F filing. Harris and Muller use regressions of market value, price-per-shares and return models on firms' earnings and book value measured under both IAS and US GAAP reconciliation amounts and find that the US GAAP earnings reconciliation adjustments are value relevant after controlling for IAS amounts only for market and returns models. They fail to find a significant association between reconciliation amounts and price-per-shares. Their tests of a greater association between market values and either IAS or US GAAP are also inconclusive. In fact, IAS amounts are more highly associated with price-per-share than US GAAP amounts, whereas US GAAP are more highly associated with security returns than IAS amounts.

The mixed results provided by Harris and Muller highlight how methodology issues matter in empirical research.

Bandyopadhyay, Hanna and Richardson (1994) find that the reconciliations do not appear to be value relevant for a set of Canadian firms listed in the US. They provide two explanations for this result. First, the reconciliation items might be the result of events that do not have a continuing effect on a firm's future cash flows, and therefore they are not impounded in price in the same way as earnings changes of a continuing nature. Alternatively, financial markets could predict the reconciliation numbers sufficiently early and prices might impound any value relevant information prior to its release.

Likewise, Barth and Clinch (1996) investigate US GAAP reconciliations for a sample of UK, Australian and Canadian firms and find that reconciliations reflect information useful to investors for the UK and Australian firms and to, a more limited extent, for Canadian firms. Given that US GAAP and Canadian GAAP are similar for many items, findings suggest that the usefulness of reconciliations to US GAAP decreases as the foreign GAAP are more closely comparable to US GAAP.

Chan and Seow (1996), instead, find that earnings based on foreign GAAP are more closely related to contemporaneous stock returns than earnings reconciled to US GAAP. Earnings based on foreign GAAP seem therefore to convey information that is lost in the reconciliation to the US GAAP. They also provide early evidence that such results could be driven by institutional factors which are specific to foreign markets. By using the returns correlation of foreign stock indexes and the Standard and Poor 500 index as a surrogate for the closeness of the foreign business environment to that of the US, Chan and Seow show that the association between stock returns and earnings based on foreign GAAP is stronger than earnings based on US GAAP for both high- and low-correlation groups, but within-group differences are much stronger for the low-correlation group than for the high-correlation group. This result suggests that foreign GAAP might reflect specific features relevant to that foreign country such as tax structures, inter-corporate ownership, industrial relations, type of economy (agriculture-based, resource-based, manufacturing) and national economic and social policies.

5. The relative informativeness of different accounting standard sets: Stakeholder versus shareholder models

As greater emphasis has been placed on accounting harmonization worldwide, knowledge of the relative informativeness of financial statements prepared according to shareholder or stakeholder model has been considered of great importance in the policy debate.

Alford *et al.* (1993) have provided early evidence on the importance of national accounting differences. Their research is based on a comparison of information content and timeliness of accounting earnings in several countries and uses the United States as a benchmark.

By regressing 15-month returns on annual earnings for each of their sample countries and using the regressions' R-square as a measure of information content, Alford *et al.* document significant differences in the timeliness and information content of accounting earnings across the sample countries. The association between earnings and stock returns is stronger in countries where capital is traditionally raised in capital markets and there are weaker links between financial and tax reporting, that is, in Anglo-Saxon countries. In addition, unconsolidated earnings are not as value relevant as consolidated earnings are.

In particular, earnings from Australia, France, The Netherlands and the United Kingdom appear to be more informative or timelier than US accounting earnings, whereas results for Belgium, Canada, Hong Kong, Ireland, Japan, Norway, South Africa and Switzerland are inconclusive. In contrast, annual accounting earnings from Denmark, Germany, Italy, Singapore, and Sweden reflect less timely or less value relevant information than US accounting earnings. Taken as a whole, these results are in line with Barth and Clinch (1996).

In the same vein, Ball, Kothari and Robin (2000) examine the effects of institutional factors on properties of accounting earnings by focusing on timeliness and conservatism of earnings reported by firms in common-law countries and code-law countries. Their idea is that the politicization of accounting standard setting and the enforcement typical of code-law countries weakened the demand for timely and conservative accounting income.

In code-law countries, political influence on accounting occurs at national and firm levels. Governments establish and enforce national accounting standards, typically with representation from major political groups such as labour unions, banks and business associations. At the firm level, politicization typically leads to a stakeholder governance model, involving agents from major groups contracting with the firm. As a consequence, current-period accounting income is to be viewed as a pie to be divided among groups, as dividends to shareholders, taxes to governments and bonuses to managers and sometimes also to employees. Furthermore, since these groups' agents are usually represented in corporate governance, insider communication is considered as a means for solving the information asymmetry between managers and stakeholders. Demand for accounting income under code law is therefore expected to be more influenced by the payout preferences of agents for labour, capital and government than in common-law countries. Their preferences are also expected to penalize volatility in payouts and, consequently, in income.

Conversely, under the shareholder governance model – which is typical of common-law countries – shareholders alone elect members of the board, payouts are less closely linked to current-period accounting income and public disclosure is a solution for the information asymmetry problem. In comparison with the more political process in code-law countries, the desirable properties of accounting income in common law countries are expected to be determined primarily in the disclosure market. Those properties include timeliness in incorporating negative economic income (i.e. asymmetric conservatism).

Empirical results support these hypotheses by showing that accounting income in common-law countries is significantly timelier than in code-law countries and incorporate economic losses quicker. Considering timeliness and conservatism together as capturing much of the concept of financial statement "transparency", Ball *et al.* conclude that these results provide an explanation for the emergence of a largely common-law model in international accounting and, in particular, for the IASB adoption of a more common-law approach to disclosure.

Similar results are provided by Ali and Hwang (2000) who investigate the relation between value relevance and country-specific factors. Their study documents that value relevance of financial reports is lower for countries where the financial system is bank-oriented rather than market-oriented; where private sector bodies are not involved in standard setting process; where accounting practices follow the Continental model as opposed to the British-American model; where tax rules have a greater influence on financial accounting measurements; and where spending on auditing services is relatively low.

Taken as a whole, research has therefore documented that financial statements prepared under the shareholder model provide better information than financial statements prepared under the stakeholder model. However, it has been unable to disentangle the effects of accounting standards from other institutional factors such as shareholders' protection or market development.

Some studies have focused specifically on a comparison between German GAAP, on the one side, and US GAAP or IAS, on the other side, as they represent relative extremes in their approaches to financial reporting. German GAAP traditionally focuses on stakeholders and uses a "prudent" approach in financial reporting, whereas US GAAP and IAS are more shareholder-oriented. Germany also has a strong legal system in terms of rule of law and efficiency in the judicial system which ensures an adequate enforcement of accounting rules (La Porta *et al.* 1998). This fact was therefore expected to increase the power of empirical tests based on German samples.

Harris *et al.* (1994), for instance, compare the relative informativeness of accounting measures for US and German firms matched on industry and firm size and find mixed results. On the one hand, the correlation between returns and annual earnings reported under German GAAP is similar to that in the United States. Further, the coefficient applied to earnings in Germany is larger than that in the United States, which is consistent with a more conservative measurement approach in Germany.

On the other hand, the regression of price on both earnings and shareholders' equity show that the explanatory power of accounting measures for price is significantly lower in Germany than in the United States. According to the authors, this could be a result of the perception that the cumulative effects on shareholders' equity of conservative accounting practices, applied over many years, have increased the uncertainty of its relevance.

Differentiating between German firms on the basis of the degrees of consolidation (parent-only, domestic-only consolidation and full consolidation), Harris *et al.* also document that the association between earnings and returns is stronger for firms that consolidate than for those that did not, consistent with the notion that consolidation increases value relevance.

Finally, they compare the explanatory power and information content of reported earnings with earnings adjusted on a formula used by analysts to derive a "permanent earnings" number, that is, earnings free of idiosyncratic economic or accounting transactions. Their findings show that the relation between returns and adjusted earnings is stronger than for reported earnings, thus suggesting an incremental informativeness of the former.

Bartov *et al.* (2005) focus only on firms reporting consolidated financial statements under German GAAP, US GAAP or IAS traded within the German market so as to hold constant institutional factors such as listing requirements, other disclosure requirements, regulatory environmental and other market microstructure factors which could confound results.

In Germany, a relatively large number of German firms adopted IAS already in the 1990s, which provided researchers with a reasonably large sample of IAS adopters. German listed firms could in fact prepare their consolidated financial statements according to internationally accepted accounting standards instead of German accounting standards. In addition, in 1997 Germany's New Market, the European equivalent of the US NASDAQ was launched to help small high-tech companies to raise equity. All companies listed on the New Market were required to use either US GAAP or IAS. This allowed researchers to investigate the value relevance of different accounting standard sets in the German stock market only, thus holding institutional factors constant.

Instead of assessing the value relevance of different accounting measures by comparing R-squares, Bartov *et al.* investigate the information content of earnings by introducing, into the regressions of returns on earnings, an accounting standard dummy variable and its product with earnings, which are supposed to reflect the differential effect of reporting earnings under US GAAP or IAS over German requirements. Results show that both US GAAP and IAS have superior value relevance in comparison with German GAAP. Furthermore, a comparison between value relevance of earnings produced under US GAAP and IAS generates evidence indicating the superiority of the former.

Gassen and Sellhorn (2006) also analyze the IAS/IFRS adoption by publicly traded German firms during the period 1998–2004 and document significant differences in terms of earnings quality. IAS/IFRS adopters show more persistent, less predictable and more conditionally conservative earnings. They also experience a decline in bid-ask spreads even though stock prices result to be more volatile.

Along the same line, Jermakowicz *et al.* (2007) find that adopting either IAS/IFRS or US GAAP or cross-listing on the NYSE significantly increases the value relevance of earnings for a sample of German firms listed on the German blue-chip stock-market.

In contrast, Hung and Subramanyan (2007) provide little evidence that the IAS/IFRS adoption improves the relative value relevance of accounting data. By regressing stock market prices on book values and net income, Hung and Subramanayan document that book value and income are no more value relevant under IAS/IFRS than under German GAAP and that IAS/IFRS income exhibits greater conditional conservatism than German GAAP income. Therefore, they conclude that there are no significant differences in value relevance between stakeholder-oriented (i. e. German GAAP) and shareholder-oriented (i. e. IAS/IFRS) accounting models. Their results are however consistent with Ball *et al.* (2000), who show that institutional factors such as shareholder protection may play a more important role than accounting standards in explaining cross-country variation in the valuation properties of accounting data.

In conclusion, research which focuses on German firms applying either German GAAP, or IAS, or US GAAP has the advantage that it investigates the effects of accounting differences under *ceteris paribus* condition. Nevertheless, results are controversial. One explanation could be related to methodological issues. For instance, the regression model by Bartov *et al.* does not include the book value of equity. Book value could therefore be an omitted variable correlated with earnings which biased coefficient on earnings (Soderstrom and Sun 2007). The inconsistent results could also arise from the use of different samples. For instance, the sample in Bartov *et al.* is larger than in Hung and Subramanyan and includes all firms traded on German stock exchanges during the 1999–2000 period. The sample in the Hung and Subramanyan consists, instead, of 80 German industrial firms adopting IAS for the first time during the 1998–2002 period.

An original analysis on the relative informativeness of domestic GAAP versus IAS or US GAAP is provided by Ashbaugh and Davis-Friday (2002), who investigate the association between non-US firms' financial reporting in accordance with IAS or US GAAP and the likelihood of such firms being targets in mergers and acquisitions. Transparent financial information is a necessary element for economic growth as market participants depend on informative and useful financial information in making capital allocation decisions (Rajan and Zingales, 1998). If the role of financial reporting is to reduce asymmetric information and financial information generated under IAS or US GAAP is more informative and more useful in determining the value of firms' resources than financial information generated under non-US firms' domestic accounting standards, then a stronger association between firms reporting in accordance with IAS or US GAAP and their likelihood of being targets in mergers and acquisitions has to be expected. The association between non-US firms' reporting of IAS or US GAAP financial information and the likelihood of firms being targets is tested for a sample of 186 non-US firms listed on the international Stock Exchange Automated Quotation System (SEAQ) in London. Ashbaugh and Davis-Friday document a positive and significant association between firms reporting IAS or US GAAP financial information and their being targets in completed mergers and acquisitions. They also find a positive and significant association between firms' external monitoring, as proxied by the firm contracting with a Big-6 auditor, and firms being targets. In addition, they focus on firms domiciled in countries which are different from their acquiring firms, that is, on cross-border mergers and acquisitions, in order to investigate whether the role of firms' financial reporting is more important when target and acquiring firms operate in differential information environments. Consistent with their original analysis, results of the cross-border analysis indicate that non-US firms' use of IAS or US GAAP is positively associated with firms being targets in cross-border mergers and acquisitions. Evidence supporting this hypothesis is also consistent with the theory that firms' financial reporting strategies have an influence on the control of corporate resources in the global market.

6. IAS/IFRS versus US GAAP

Many market observers, practitioners, researchers, and regulators have argued that financial statements prepared under US GAAP provide better information than IAS/IFRS as the former are more rigorously defined (Bartov *et al.* 2005). Several studies have therefore focused on the relative informativeness of IAS/IFRS and US GAAP in order to assess which of the them is more useful to investors.

This is a key issue in the worldwide converging process. European Regulation 1606/2002 states in fact that

> [...] it is important for the competitiveness of capital markets to achieve convergence [...] This implies an increasing convergence of accounting standards currently used internationally with the ultimate objective of achieving a single set of global accounting standards.

As mentioned above, Harris and Muller (1999) is the first study comparing the relative informativeness of IAS and US GAAP. They use the Form 20-F to directly and specifically compare the association between firm value and IAS and US GAAP accounting measures as they were implemented by foreign firms listed in US. They regress market value, price-per-shares and return models on firms' earnings and book value measured under IAS and US GAAP reconciliation amounts and find mixed results. Findings show in fact that US GAAP earnings reconciliation adjustments are value relevant after controlling for IAS amounts for market and returns models, whereas significant association between reconciliation amounts and price-per-shares is found. Their tests of a greater association between market values and either IAS or US GAAP are also inconclusive. In fact, IAS amounts are more highly associated with price-per-share than US GAAP amounts, whereas US GAAP are more highly associated with security.

Gordon *et al.* (2010) and Hughes and Sander (2007) also compare earnings attributes for earnings based both on IAS/IFRS and on US GAAP-reconciled amounts. These studies generally find that IAS/IFRS and US GAAP-reconciled earnings are comparable, although there is some evidence that US GAAP-reconciled earnings are of higher quality.

Bartov *et al.* (2005) also make a comparison between value relevance of earnings produced under US GAAP and IAS/IFRS by firms listed on the German *Neuer* Market and find that US GAAP exhibited a superior value relevance than IAS/IFRS.

Examining the factors associated with 211 firms listed on the London Stock Exchange in 1993 voluntarily applying IAS/IFRS or US GAAP, Ashbaugh (2001) shows that firms are more likely to adopt IAS/IFRS when participating in seasoned equity offerings and when IAS/IFRS are less costly to implement because they require fewer accounting policy changes from domestic GAAP relative to US GAAP. Instead, the adoption of US GAAP is mainly driven by the SEC filing requirements faced by firms.

More recently, the debate on the relative informativeness of IAS/IFRS and US GAAP has been revived by possible use of IAS/IFRS by US firms. Following its 2007 decisions to permit non-US firms cross-listing in the US to file financial statements based on IAS/IFRS, SEC is presently considering permitting also US firms to file financial statements based on IFRS.

Using a sample of firms domiciled in 27 countries that adopted IAS/IFRS between 1995 and 2006 on a matched sample of US firms, Barth *et al.* (2011) find that IAS/IFRS firms have significantly greater value relevance comparability with US firms when they applied IFRS than when they applied non-US domestic standards. In addition, comparability is significantly greater for firms that adopted IAS/IFRS mandatorily, for firm-year observations after 2005, and for IAS/IFRS firms domiciled in countries with common law legal origin and with high enforcement. These findings suggest therefore that effects from converging accounting standards and the increasing mandatory use of IAS/IFRS throughout the world have actually increased comparability of accounting numbers.

Additional findings also indicate that although US firms' accounting amounts generally have higher value relevance than those of IAS/IFRS firms, IAS/IFRS-based accounting amounts are comparable to US GAAP-based accounting amounts for firms from common law legal origin countries and from high enforcement countries. IAS/IFRS lead in fact to lower quality financial numbers when firms outside the US are subject to different reporting incentives. This provides evidence of the importance of legal systems and firms' incentives in the enforcement of accounting rules.

Van der Meulen *et al.* (2007) focus on German firms listed on Neuer Market and explore differences between US GAAP and IAS/IFRS by testing two market-based earnings attributes, i.e., value relevance and timeliness, as well as two accounting-based earnings attributes, i.e., predictability and accrual quality. Findings show that US GAAP and IAS/IFRS perform equally well on value relevance, timeliness and accruals quality, whereas US GAAP are superior with regard to predictive ability. This result also holds after controlling for differences in firm characteristics, such as size, leverage and the audit firm.

Finally, an original analysis by Ashbaugh and Olsson (2002) provide insight into differences between IAS/IFRS and US GAAP in terms of their valuation properties. Using non-US/non UK firms listed on the International Stock Exchange Automated Quotation System (SEAQ) in London, they show that the earnings capitalization model is the dominant valuation model when valuing IAS/IFRS firms' shares. The book value and the residual income models do not perform as well, as their exploratory power is weaker and the magnitude of the coefficient indicates model misspecification. A possible explanation for such results is that discretionary accounting measurement and recognition methods under IAS/IFRS violate the residual income assumptions (e.g. revaluation of fixed assets). At the same time, they identify measurement and recognition methods under IAS/IFRS (e.g. capitalization of development costs) that likely contribute to the dominance of the earnings capitalization model for IAS/IFRS firms. Conversely, the residual income model results to be the dominant valuation model for cross-listed firms reporting under US GAAP. The residual income model is well specified, whereas the estimated parameters of the earnings capitalization and book value models indicate misspecification.

7. The harmonization process in the European Union: The fourth and seventh directives

One of the fundamental objectives of the European Union is the freedom of establishment for firms and the free movement of capital, which requires a common environment under which firms conduct their business. Accounting legislation has also been part of the company law harmonization program, which provided a framework and a set of minimum requirements that member states should implement.

Similarly to the legislation in many other fields, financial markets and disclosure have normally been regulated by directives. After adoption, which is the result of a usually lengthy process that involves the European Commission, the European Parliament, and the Council of Ministers of the member states, a directive commits member states to incorporate the provisions in the directive into national law within a certain period. Another legislative instrument is a regulation that is directly effective without requiring the transposition into national law. While it had not been generally used to regulate financial disclosure, this instrument gained popularity when important regulatory actions were enacted by regulations, notably the requirement in Regulation 1606/2002 that listed corporations use IAS/IFRS in their consolidated statements.

The Fourth Directive, enacted in 1978, and the Seventh Directive, enacted in 1983, were the most influential acts in the European Union relative to financial reporting. The Fourth Directive dealt with the accounts of limited liability companies, whereas the Seventh Directive contained rules for consolidated statements. Both Directives propelled significant changes in company legislation in the European member states.

The Fourth Directive specified "true and fair view" as an overriding principle of financial reporting and defined the format and measurement of balance sheets and income statements.

The Seventh Directive addressed issues associated with consolidation. It set forth requirements for consolidation and applied the true and fair view to consolidated financial statements.

The Directives addressing financial disclosure generated several major achievements in harmonization. For example, they achieved some convergence in the objectives of financial reporting ("the true and fair view") and auditing in general. Consolidated financial statements were introduced in several member states that had not previously required them and the consolidation methods of those states that already required consolidated statements converged. The Directives also reached a compromise between the different legal approaches found in the member states, most notably the legalistic approach, as in Germany, and the common law approach, as in the United Kingdom.

The objective of the Directives was to harmonize financial disclosure, that is, to reduce the number of differences in accounting standards, across the European Union member states. However, harmonization did not require that the same rules be applied in all member states, but that the prevailing rules were compatible with those in other member states. The Directives included in fact optional rules. The Fourth Directive, for instance, included some 60 and the Seventh Directive some 50 options. There were dozens of provisions in the Fourth Directive that began with such expressions as "member states may require or permit companies to…". They represent various accounting methods followed in the member states, such as for valuation bases (cost or fair value) and accounting for goodwill. Even in the area of the disclosure layout, which was a major element regulated by the Directives, there were various forms for the presentation of the balance sheet and the income statement. There was no requirement to draw up a cash flow statement, and segment reporting required only the breakdown of sales with respect to business and geographical segments. Therefore, the enacted accounting rules in the member states continued to be quite different and the accounting practices were even more different.

The exact effects of the Fourth and Seventh Directives on a particular country depended upon the laws passed by national legislatures. Given this flexibility, the effects of the accounting Directives differed from country to country.

A comparison of the detailed rules governing financial disclosure across European countries shows that diversity persisted (d'Arcy and Ordelheide, 2001). A simulation by Simmonds and Aziéres (1989) of a hypothetical company's reported income under different countries' accounting standards in 1989 shows that the reported net income ranges from some 20 to 200 million ECU (European Currency Unit, a predecessor to the Euro), with the average around 130 to 150 million ECU.

In the same vein, the study by Bae, Tan and Welker (2008) provides a clear picture of the differences in accounting standards across European countries. They identify differences between domestic standards and IAS/IFRS, which are used as a benchmark, on 21 accounting rules for a sample of 49 countries. For the European countries, the number of accounting rules that they find to vary with respect to IFRS range from just one, in the case of the United Kingdom and Ireland, to 18 for Luxemburg.

In the accounting literature, most of the discussion on the European Directives has been normative and has focused on the desirability of the changes (Walton 1992), on alternate approaches to integrating capital market (Wilson 1991) and on the potential definitions of abstract concepts such as "true and fair view" (Alexander 1993, Walton 1993, Ordelheide 1993, Burlaud 1993, Van Hulle and Leuven 1993). Other studies have empirically analysed the effects of these Directives, but only in terms of a reduction in the variability of accounting practices within countries (Walton 1992, Emenyonu and Gray 1992). Empirical research on the capital market effects of the European Directives is therefore very scarce.

Joos and Lang (1994) provide the first empirical analysis of the impact of the European Directives on capital markets. They investigate the market impact of accounting harmonization across France, Germany and the UK by comparing different financial ratios and stock market valuations of accounting data in the period before and after the implementation of the Directives.

The effect of diversity in measurement practices across countries is evaluated either on the basis of convergence in accounting-based measure of profitability – return of equity (ROE) – and price multiples – earnings/price ratio (E/P) and book-to-market ratio (B/M) –, or by assessing the degree of association between accounting data – earnings and book value – and stock prices. The strength of the association, as measured by the R-squares, provides insight into the value relevance of the accounting measures.

Because part of the decision to move EU accounting methods closer to those for the UK is based on the alleged superior value relevance of the UK accounting principles, Joos and Lang expect to see stronger association between earnings and returns for Germany and France in the post-directive period. Moreover, as the Directives reduced differences across countries, they expect convergence in the R-squares during the post-directive period, with Germany and France moving toward the UK.

Results, however, do not provide any evidence that measurement practices in the UK result in accounting data with a higher association with share price, which is inconsistent with the arguments underlying the decision to move EU accounting requirements toward those in the UK. Neither do they find evidence of significant convergence in R-square during the post-directives period. Given the similarity of the underlying economies, Joos and Lang attribute this finding to the flexibilities still allowed by the Directives in adopting different accounting approaches, which left substantial differences in accounting among Germany, France and the UK. As mentioned, while the Directives required those financial statements to reflect the "true and fair value", their more specific requirements, particularly on measurement issues, left discretion to member states, thus leading some commentators (Alexander and Archer 1991; Walton 1992) to speculate that the changes may have represented more form than substance.

This led Joos and Lang to conclude that, "to the extent that comparable measurement of net income and shareholders' equity is perceived as important, additional attempts at integration may be merited".

Ding *et al.* (2007) also investigate European cross-country differences in domestic accounting standards by using IAS/IFRS as a benchmark. They show that dissimilarities vary according to the importance of country equity markets. In fact, differences are larger in countries with less developed capital markets, where banks supply most of the capital needs of business and have direct access to company information. On the contrary, differences are smaller for countries with more-developed capital markets, where firms receive most of their financing from small shareholders, who rely on public information for their decisions.

In conclusion, the research on European cross-country differences in domestic accounting standards after the Fourth and Seventh Directives shows that their implementation has been widely affected by the overall institutional setting, including the legal and political system of the country. Research has therefore provided useful insight into the difficulties related to the purpose of the Directives to unify the conceptual framework of financial reporting in the European Union. An additional attempt in this direction has been represented by the European Union Regulation No. 1606/2002, which has standardized accounting standards by mandating IAS/IFRS for all European listed companies from 2005 on.

References

Adams, C.A., P. Weetman and S.J. Gray (1993), "Reconciling national with international accounting standards. Lessons from a study of Finish corporate reports", *European Accounting Review*, 2(3), 471–494.

Alexander, D. and S. Archer (1991), *European accounting guide*, San Diego, CA, Harcourt Brace.

Alexander, D. (1993), "A European true and fair view?", *European Accounting Review*, 2(1), 17–46.

Alexander, D. (1993), "A European true and fair view?", *European Accounting Review*, 2(1), 59–80.

Alford, A., J. Jones, R. Leftwitch and M. Zmijeski (1993), "The relative informativeness of accounting disclosure in different countries", *Journal of Accounting Research*, 31, Supplement, 183–223.

Ali, A. and P. Zarowin (1992), "The role of earnings levels in annual earnings-returns studies", *Journal of Accounting Research,* 30, 286–296.

Ali, A. and L.-S. Hwang (2000), "Country-specific factors related to financial reporting and the value relevance of accounting data", *Journal of Accounting Research*, 38(1), 1–21.

Amir, E., T.S. Harris, and E.K. Venuti (1993), "A Comparison of the Value-Relevance of U.S. Versus Non-U.S. GAAP Accounting Measures Using Form 20-F Reconciliations", *Journal of Accounting Research*, 31, 230–264.

Ampofoa, A. and R. Sellani (2005), "Examining the differences between United States Generally Accepted Accounting principles (US GAAP) and International Accounting Standards (IAS): implications for the harmonization of accounting standards", *Accounting Forum*, 29, 219–231.

André, P., D. Dionysiou, I. Tsalavoutas and D. Yang (2011), *Accounting comparability: a literature review*. Working paper, Paris, ESSEC Business School.

Archibald, T. Ross (1972), "Stock Market Reaction to the Depreciation Switch-Rule", *The Accounting Review*, XLVII, January, 22–30.

Ashbaugh, H. (1999), *The cost and benefits associated with firms' application of IAS: a longitudinal study*. Working paper.

Ashbaugh, H. (2001), "Non-US firms' accounting standard choices", *Journal of Accounting and Public Policy,* 20, 129–153.

Ashbaugh, H. and M. Pincus (2001), "Domestic accounting standards, International Accounting Standards, and the predictability of earnings", *Journal of Accounting Research,* 39, 417–434.

Ashbaugh, H. and P. Olsson (2002), "An Exploratory Study of the Valuation Properties of Cross-Listed Firms' IAS and U.S. GAAP Earnings and Book Values", *The Accounting Review*, LXXVII, 107–126.

Ashbaugh, H. and P. Y. Davis-Friday (2002), *The role of non-US firms' financial reporting in international mergers & acquisitions.* Working paper, University of Wisconsin-Madison.

Atiase, R. and L. Bamber (1994), "Trading Volume Reactions to Annual Accounting Earnings Announcements", *Journal of Accounting and Economics,* May, 309–329.

Bae, K.-H., H. Tan and M. Welker (2008), "International GAAP differences: the impact on foreign analysts", *The Accounting Review*, 83(3), 593–628.

Baiman, S. and R. Verrecchia (1996), "The Relation among Capital Markets, Financial Disclosure, Production Efficiency, and Insider Trading", *Journal of Accounting Research,* Spring, 1–22.

Baker, R. and E. Barbu (2007), "Trends in research on international accounting harmonization", *The International Journal of Accounting,* 42, 272–304.

Ball, R., and P. Brown (1968), "An Empirical Evaluation of Accounting Income Numbers", *Journal of Accounting research,* 6, 159–178.

Ball, R., S. P. Kothari, and A. Robin (2000), "The effect of international institutional factors on properties of accounting earnings", *Journal of Accounting and Economics,* 29, 1–51.

Ball, R., A. Robin and J. Wu (2003), "Incentives versus standards: properties of accounting income in four East Asian countries", *Journal of Accounting and Economics,* 36, 235–270.

Ball, R. (2006), "IFRS: pros and cons for investors", *Accounting and Business Research,* International Accounting Policy Forum, 5–27.

Bandyopadhyay, S. P., J. D. Hanna and G. Richardson (1994), "Capital market effects of American-Canadian GAAP differences", *Journal of Accounting Research,* 32, 262–277.

Barth, M. E. and G. Clinch (1996), "International differences in accounting standards: evidence from UK, Australian, and Canadian firms", *Contemporary Accounting Research,* Spring, 135–170.

Barth, M. E., W. H. Beaver and W. R. Landsman (2001), "The relevance of the value relevance literature for financial accounting standard setting: another view", *Journal of Accounting and Economics,* 31, 77–104.

Barth, M. E. (2007), "Standard-setting measurement issues and the relevance of research", *Accounting and Business Research,* Special Issue: International Accounting Policy Forum, 7–15.

Barth, M., W. Landsman and M. Lang (2008), "International Accounting Standards and accounting quality", *Journal of Accounting Research,* 46(3), 467–498.

Barth, M., W. Landsman, M. Lang and C. Williams (2011), *Are International Accounting Standards-based and US GAAP-based accounting amounts comparable? Journal of Accounting and Economics.* Working paper, Stanford University and University of North Carolina.

Bartov, E. and G. Bodnar (1996), "Alternative Accounting Methods, Information Asymmetry and Liquidity: Theory and Evidence", *The Accounting Review,* July, 397–418.

Bartov, E., S. Goldberg and M. Kim (2005), "Comparative value relevance among German, U.S. and International Accounting Standards: A German stock market perspective", *Journal of Accounting, Auditing and Finance,* 20, 95–119.

Baumol, W. and B. Malkiel (1993), "Redundant regulation of foreign security trading and U.S. competitiveness", *Journal of Applied Corporate Finance.*

BDO, D.T. Tohmatsu, E. Young, G. Thornton, KPMG and P. Coopers (2003), *GAAP 2001, a survey of national efforts to promote and achieve convergence with international financial reporting standards.*

Beaver, W.H., J.W. Kennelly and W.M. Voss (1968), "Predictive Ability as a Criterion for the Evaluation of Accounting Data", *The Accounting Review*, 675–683.

Beaver, W.H., R. Clarke and W.F. Wright (Autumn, 1979), "The Association Between Unsystematic Security Returns and The Magnitude of Earnings Forecast Errors", *Journal of Accounting Research,* 316–340.

Beaver, W.H. (AAA, 1972), "The Behavior of Security Prices and its Implications for Accounting Research (Methods)", *Committee Reports: Supplements to Volume XLVII of Accounting Review,* 407–437.

Beckers, S., R. Grinold and A. Rudd (1992), "The relative importance of common factors across the European equity markets", *Journal of Banking and Finance*, 16, 75–95.

Benston, G.J., M. Bromwich, R.E. Litan and A. Wagenhofer (2006), *Worlwide financial reporting. The development and future of accounting standards*, Oxford, Oxford University Press.

Biddle, G.C. and S.M. Saudagaran (1989), "The effects of financial disclosure levels on firms' choices among alternative foreign stock exchange listings", *Journal of International Financial Management and Accounting,* 1, 55–87.

Biddle, G.C., G.S. Seow and A.F. Siegel (1995), "Relative versus incremental information content", *Contemporary Accounting Research*, 12, 1–23.

Black, F. (1980), "The Magic in Earnings: Economic Earnings versus Accounting Earnings", *Financial Analysts' Journal,* November/December, 19–24.

Boone, J. (1998), "Oil and Gas Reserve Value Disclosures and Bid-Ask Spreads", *Journal of Accounting and Public Policy,* Spring, 55–84.

Bowman R.G. (1980), "The Debt Equivalence of Leases: An Empirical Investigation", *The Accounting Review,* April.

Burgstahler, D. and I. Dichev (1997), "Earnings, adaptation, and equity value", *The Accounting Review*, 72, 187–215.

Burlaud, A. (1993), "Commentaires sur l'article de David Alexander 'A European true and fair view?'", *European Accounting Review*, 2(1), 91–94.

Burlaud, A. (1993), "Commentary on the article by David Alexander 'A European true and fair view?'", *European Accounting Review*, 2(1), 95–98.

Bushee, B. and C. Noe (2000), "Disclosure Quality, Institutional Invenstors, and Stock Return Volatility", *Journal of Accounting Research*, supplement, 171–202.

Chan, K. C. and G. S. Seow (1996), "The association between stock returns and foreign GAAP earnings versus earnings adjusted to US-GAAP", *Journal of Accounting and Economics*, 21, 139–158.

Chua, W. and S. Taylor (2008), "The rise and rise of IFRS: an examination of IFRS diffusion", *Journal of Accounting and Public Policy*, 27, 462–473.

D'Arcy, A. and D. Ordelheide (2001), "A reference matrix" in Ordelheide, D. and KPMG, eds. *Transnational Accounting*, 2nd ed., Houndmills, Basingstoke, UK and New York, Palgrave, 1–101.

D'Arcy, A. (2001), "Hat sich die internationale Bilanzierung für den Neuen Markt bewährt?" in Coenenberg, A. G. and K. Pohle, eds., *Internationale Rechnungslegung*, Stuttgart, Schäffer-Poeschel, 165–177.

Delvaille, P., G. Ebbers and C. Saccon (2005), "International Financial Reporting convergence: evidence from three continental European countries", *Accounting in Europe*, 2(1), 137–164.

Ding, Y., T. Jeanjean and H. Stolowy (2005), "Why do national GAAP differ from IAS? The role of culture", *The International Journal of Accounting*, 40, 325–350.

Ding, Y., O.-K. Hope, T. Jeanjean and H. Stolowy (2007), "Differences between domestic accounting standards and IAS: Measurement, determinants and implications", *Journal of Accounting and Public Policy*, 26, 1–38.

Edwards, F. R. (1993), "Listing of foreign securities on US exchanges", *Journal of Applied Corporate Finance*, 5, 28–36.

Emenyonu, E. and S. Gray (1992), "EC accounting harmonisation: an empirical study of measurement practices in France, Germany and the UK", *Accounting and Business Research*, 23(89), 49–58.

Erickson, D., A. Esplin and L. Maines (2009), "One world-one accounting", *Business Horizons*, 52, 531–537.

Gammie, M., S. Giannini, A. Lemm, A. Oestreicher, P. Parascandolo and C. Spengel (2005), *Achieving a common consolidated corporate tax base in the EU*, Brussels, CEPS.

Gassen, J. and T. Selhorn (2006), "Applying IFRS in Germany – determinants and consequences", *Betriebswirtschaftliche Forschung und Praxis*, 58(3).

Givoly, D. and J. Lakonishok (1979), "The Information Content of Financial Analysts' Forecasts of Earnings", *Journal of Accounting and Economics*, 1, 165–185.

Gjerde, O., K. Knivsfla and F. Saettem (2008), "The value-relevance of adopting IFRS: evidence from 145 NGAAP restatements", *Journal of International Accounting, Auditing and Taxation*, 17, 92–112.

Gordon., E. A., B. N. Jorgensen and C. L. Linthicum (2010), *Could IFRS replace US GAAP? A comparison of earnings attributes and informativeness in the US market.* Working paper.

Guerreiro, M., L. Lima Rodrigues and R. Craig (2008), "The preparedness of companies to adopt International Financial reporting Standards: Portuguese evidence", *Accounting Forum*, 32, 75–88.

Haller, A. (2002), "Financial accounting developments in the European Union: past events and future prospects", *European Accounting Review*, 11(1), 153–190.

Harris, T., M. Lang, and H. P. Moeller (1994), "The value relevance of German accounting measures: An empirical analysis", *Journal of Accounting Research*, 32(2), 187–209.

Harris, T. (1995), *International accounting standards versus US-GAAP reporting: empirical evidence based on case studies*, Cincinnati OH, International Thompson Press.

Harris, M.S. and K.A. Muller III (1999), "The market valuation of IAS versus US GAAP accounting measures using Form 20-F reconciliation", *Journal of Accounting and Economics*, 26, 285–312.

Hayn, C. (1995), "The information Content of Losses", *Journal of Accounting and Economics*, 20, 125–153.

Haverty, J. (2006), "Are IFRS and US GAAP converging? Some evidence from people's Republic of China companies listed on the New York Stock Exchange", *Journal of International Accounting, Auditing and Taxation*, 15, 48–71.

Healy, P., A. Hutton and K. Palepu (1999), "Stock performance and intermediation changes surrounding sustained increases in disclosure", *Contemporary Accounting Research*, 16, 485–520.

Hellman, N. (1993), "A comparative analysis of the impact of accounting differences on profits and return on equity. Differences between Swedish practice and US GAAP", *European Accounting Review*, 2(3), 495–530.

Holthausen, R.W. and R.L. Watts (2001), "The relevance of the value-relevance literature for financial accounting standard setting", *Journal of Accounting and Economics*, 31, 3–75.

Horton, J. and G. Serafeim (2010), "Market reaction to and valuation of IFRS reconciliation adjustments: first evidence from the UK", *Review of Accounting Studies*, 15(4), 725–751.

Hughes, S.B. and J.F. Sander (2007), *Are IFRSs and US GAAP converging? Preliminary evidence from three European Union countries*. Working paper.

Hung, M. and K. Subramanyam (2007), "Financial statement effects of adopting International Accounting Standards: The case of Germany", *Review of Accounting Studies*, 12, 623–657.

Jaruga, A. (1993), "Changing rules of accounting in Poland", *European Accounting Review*, 2(1), 115–126.

Joos, P. and M. Lang (1994), "The effects of accounting diversity: Evidence from the European Union", *Journal of Accounting Research*, 32, 141–168.

Kenny, S.Y. and Larson R.K. (1993), "Lobbying behaviour and the development of international accounting standards. The case of the IASC's joint venture project", *European Accounting Review*, 2(3), 531–554.

KPMG (2000), "*Global Financial Reporting, IAS or US GAAP?*", European Survey, London.

Kaplan R. and R. Roll (1972), "Investor Evaluation of Accounting Information: Some Empirical Evidence", *Journal of Business*, April, XLV.

Kothari, S.P. (2001), "Capital markets research in accounting", *Journal of Accounting and Economics,* 31(1–3), 105–231.

La Porta, R., F. Lopez-de-Silanes, A. Shleifer and R. Vishny (1997), "Legal determinants of external finance", *The Journal of Finance,* 52, 1131–1150.

La Porta, R., F. Lopez-de-Silanes, A. Shleifer and R.W. Vishny (1998), "Law and finance", *The Journal of Political Economy,* 106(6), 1113–1155.

Lamb, M., C. Nobes and A. Roberts (1998), "International variations in the connections between tax and financial reporting", *Accounting and Business Research,* 28(3), 173–188.

Landsman, W.R. (2007), "Is fair value accounting information relevant and reliable? Evidence from capital market research", *Accounting and Business Research,* 37(3).

Lang, M. and R. Lundholm (1993), "Cross- Sectional Determinants of Analyst Rating of Corporate Disclosures", *Journal of Accounting Research,* Autumn, 246–271.

Larson, R. and D.L. Street (2004a), "Large accounting firms' survey reveals emergence of 'two standard' system in the European Union", *Advances in International Accounting,* 17, 1–29.

Larson, R. and D.L. Street (2004b), "Convergence with IFRS in an expanding Europe: progress and obstacles identified by large accounting firms' survey", *Journal of International Accounting, Auditing and Taxation,* 13, 89–119.

Leuz, C. and R.E. Verrecchia (2000), "The Economic consequences of Increased Disclosure", *Journal of Accounting Research,* 38, Supplement, 91–124.

Lev, B. and J.A. Ohlson (1982), "Market-Based Empirical Research in Accounting: A Review, Interpretation, and Extension", *Journal of Accounting Research,* 20, Supplement.

Levitt, A. (1988), "The Importance of High Quality Accounting Standards", *Accounting Horizons,* March, 79–82.

Meek, G.K. (1983), "U.S. securities market responses to alternative earnings disclosures of non-U.S. multinational corporations", *The Accounting Review,* 58, 394–402.

Meek, G.K. and S.M. Saudagaran (1990), "A survey of research on financial reporting in a transnational context", *Journal of Accounting Literature,* 9, 394–402.

Mlynarczyk, F.A. (1969), "An Empirical Study of Accounting Methods and Stock Prices", *Selected Studies, Journal of Accounting Research,* 7, supplement *Empirical Research in Accounting,* 63–81.

Nobes, C. (2003), "A conceptual framework for the taxable income of business, and how to apply it under IFRS", *Certified Accountants Educational,* London, Trust.

Nobes, C. (2004), "On accounting classification and the international harmonisation debate", *Accounting, Organizations and Society,* 29(2), 189–200.

Nobes, C. (2006), "The survival of international differences under IFRS: towards a research agenda", *Accounting and Business Research,* 36(3), 233–245.

Nobes, C. and R.B. Parker (2008), *Comparative International Accounting,* 10th edn. Prentice-Hall-Financial Times, Chapter 6.

Noreen E. and J. Sepe (1981), "Market Reaction to Accounting Policy Deliberations: The Inflation Accounting Case", *The Accounting Review,* October.
O'Donnell, J.L. (1965), "Relationships Between Reported Earnings and Stock Prices in the Electric Utility Industry", *The Accounting Review,* January, XL, 135–143.
O' Donnell, J.L. (1968), "Further Observation on Reported Earnings and Stock Prices", *The Accounting Review,* July, XLII.
Patz D. and J. Boatsman (1980), "Accounting Principle Formulation in an Efficient Market Environment", *Journal of Accounting Research,* Spring.
Ohlson J. (1995), "Earnings, book value and dividends in security valuation", *Contemporary Accounting Research",* 661–687.
Ordelheide, D. (1993), "True and fair view. A European and a German perspective", *European Accounting Review*, 2(1), 81–90.
Patz, D. and J. Boatsman (1980), "Accounting principle formulation in an efficient market environment", *Journal of Accounting Research*, Spring.
Ragan, J., J. Hadley and A. Raymond (2007), "IFRS: approaching a state of convergence", *International Business & Economics Research Journal*, 6(12), 15–24.
Rajan, R. and L. Zingales (1998), "Financial dependence and growth", *American Economic Review*, 88, 559–586.
Rees, L. and P. Elger (1997), "The market's valuation of nonreported accounting measures: retrospective reconciliations of non-US and US GAAP", *Journal of Accounting Research*, 35, 115–127.
Schipper, K. (2005), "The introduction of International Accounting Standards in Europe: implications for international convergence", *European Accounting Review*, 14(1), 101–126.
Simmonds, A. and Azières O. (1989), *Accounting for Europe: Success by 2000 AD*, London, Touche Ross.
Soderstrom, N.S. and K.J. Sun (2007), "IFRS adoption and accounting quality: a review", *European Accounting Review*, 16(4), 675–702.
Tav, J. and R.H. Parker (1990), "Measuring international harmonization and standardization", *Abacus*, 26(1), 71–88.
Tokar, M. (2005), "Convergence and the implementation of a single set of global standards: the real-life challenge", *Accounting in Europe*, 2(1), 47–68.
Van der Meulen, S.A. Gaeremynck and M. Willekens (2007), "Attribute differences between US GAAP and IFRS earnings: an explanatory study", *The International Journal of Accounting*, 42, 123–142.
Van Hulle, K. and K.U. Leuven (1993), "Truth and untruth about true and fair: a commentary on 'A European true and fair view?' comment", *European Accounting Review*, 2(1), 99–104.
Vellam, I. (2004), "Implementation of International Accounting Standards in Poland: can true convergence be achieved in practice?", *Accounting in Europe*, 1(1), 143–167.
Vigeland R.L. (1981), "The Market Reaction to Statement of Financial Accounting Standards No. 2", *Journal of Accounting Research,* Autumn.

Walton, P. (1982), "Harmonization of Accounting in France and Britain: Some Evidence", *Abacus*, 28(2), 186–199.
Walton, P. (1993), "Introduction: the true and fair view in British accounting", *European Accounting Review*, 2(1), 49–58.
Walton, P. (1993), "Company law and accounting in nineteenth-century Europe", *European Accounting Review*, 2(2), 286–291.
Walton, P. (1997), "The true and fair view and the drafting of the fourth directive", *European Accounting Review*, 6(4), 721–730.
Walton, P. (2000), "The future of the accounting profession in Europe", *European Accounting Review*, 9(4), 589–591.
Weißenberger, B., A. Stahl and S. Vorstius (2004), "Changing from German GAAP to IFRS or US GAAP: a survey of German companies", *Accounting in Europe*, 1(1), 143–167.
Welker, M. (1995), "Disclosure Policy, Information Asymmetry, and Liquidity in Equity Markets", *Contemporary Accounting Research,* Spring, 801–827.
Wilson, A. (1991), "Harmonization through equivalence", *Accountancy,* April, 81–82.
Zeff, S. (2007), "Some obstacles to global financial reporting comparability and convergence at a high level of quality", *The British Accounting Review*, 39, 290–302.

Chapter 3

The IAS/IFRS Adoption in the European Union

1. Introduction

One of the main concerns of Regulators is over the "fairness" of capital markets, which should avoid adversities and inequalities for investors stemming from informational deficiencies. From this perspective, financial reporting is expected by regulators to play a fundamental role in reducing information asymmetries.

Good financial reporting provides a favourable climate for capital markets because of its effect on the perceived fairness of such markets. Investors are more willing to invest funds in markets if there is greater disclosure and less risk of fraud or misrepresentation about the productive opportunities of the firm issuing securities. The subsequent marketability of securities is also a function of the perceived fairness of capital markets. If capital markets are efficient with respect to a rich, comprehensive information system, investors are less concerned about information asymmetries at the time they buy and sell their securities and are more willing to invest.

On the contrary, information asymmetries negatively affect capital markets with damages for economic growth, job creation and personal wealth.

Good accounting, in which markets have confidence, is a fundamental building block for successful capital markets. Good accounting rests on standards that are consistent, comprehensive and based on clear principles which enable financial reports to reflect the underlying economic reality.

Worldwide disparities in accounting requirements have been caused by a variety of social, economic and legal circumstances and by different countries keeping in mind the needs of different users of financial statements when setting national accounting standards. As mentioned previously, some countries, such as the US, have developed accounting requirements that focus more on shareholders and are based on fair value accounting. Conversely, in Europe, the Fourth and Seventh Directives have provided an accounting system that focuses more on debt holders and places greater emphasis on creditor protection. Under such Directives, accounting relies upon the historical recoverable cost criterion and mandates that prudence prevails over accrual. Furthermore, since the member states kept substantial flexibility in adopting provisions complying with the Directives into national law, a variety of domestic factors, such as tax-based incentives for accounting method choice, the desire to reduce trade unions' demands for higher wages, or shareholder demands for higher dividends, have influenced accounting method choices.

Although the purpose of the European Directives was to unify the framework of financial reporting in the European Union, research has shown that they did not achieve such a goal. As a consequence, many commentators questioned the real harmonising effect of the Directives on measurement practices and called for further integration in financial reporting.

2. European Regulation 1606/2002

One important step in the modernization process of the accounting model in Europe is represented by the European Parliament and Council Regulation No. 1606, 19 July 2002 (in appendix).

According to this Regulation, the Fourth and Seventh European Directives, on which domestic GAAP are based in Europe,

> [...] cannot ensure the high level of transparency and comparability of financial reporting from all publicly traded Community companies which is a necessary condition for building an integrated capital market which operates effectively, smoothly and efficiently. It is therefore necessary to supplement the legal framework applicable to publicly traded companies.

For this reason, "publicly traded companies must be required to apply a single set of high quality international accounting standards for the preparation of their consolidated financial statements".

As a consequence of Regulation 1606/2002, for each financial year starting on or after 1 January 2005, companies governed by the law of a member state must prepare their consolidated accounts in conformity with the international accounting standards adopted within the Community if, on their balance sheet date, their securities are admitted to trading on a regulated market of any member state. The Regulator has also provided an option for member states to permit or require the application of international accounting standards in the preparation of annual accounts and to permit or require their application by unlisted companies.

The appendix reports the state of IAS/IFRS implementation by the European Union member states at the date of February 2012.

The international accounting standards which the Regulation 1606/2002 refers to are the International Accounting Standards IAS/IFRS. Art. 2 states that

> […] for the purpose of this Regulation "international accounting standards" shall mean International Accounting Standards (IAS), International Financial Reporting Standards (IFRS) and related Interpretations (SIC-IFRIC interpretations), subsequent amendments to those standards and related interpretations, future standards and related interpretations issued or adopted by the International Accounting Standards Board (IASB).

IAS were issued by the International Accounting Standard Committee (IASC), predecessor of the International Accounting Standard Board (IASB) until 2000, while IFRS are issued by the IASB.

As the explicit purpose of Regulation 1606/2012 is to ensure a high degree of transparency and comparability of financial statements, requiring IAS/IFRS for financial reporting involves that such standards are deemed to both provide a high degree of transparency in financial statements and to ensure a high degree of comparability among financial statements of firms from different countries that previously used domestic GAAP based on the European Directives. Quality and comparability of financial reporting are therefore expected to improve after the IAS/IFRS adoption.

As stated by Regulation 1606/2002, the final goal of adopting IAS/IFRS in the European Union is to ensure an effective and efficient functioning of the capital market. A higher level of transparency in financial reporting should lower the estimation risk premium which arises from information asymmetries and, as a result, the firm's cost of capital. By enhancing comparability, the IAS/IFRS adoption at the European level should also reduce cross-country differences in the cost of capital and, therefore, foster an equal footing competition for financial resources among firms.

The IASB's approach to financial reporting is much closer to the US regulation than to the Fourth and Seventh Directives. The IASB focuses more on equity investors and conceives financial reporting in a more dynamic way, whereas the Directives have been concerned with the protection of debt holders and mandated more conservative evaluation methods. Under the Directives, prudence prevails over accrual and historical cost is the basic criterion for financial reporting.

As Mr. Tweedie clarified,

> [...] the IASB and partner standard setters are tackling some of the fundamental challenges facing accounting today in order to make the accounting model relevant. For too long, earnings have been smoothed in an effort to show investors a steady upward trajectory of profits. While this approach provides a simple and understandable model, it simply is not consistent with reality. Publicly traded companies are complex entities, engaged in a wide range of activities and subject to different market pressures and fluctuations. Accounting should reflect these fluctuations and risks. The focus on providing a steady stream of earnings only distorts the picture and encourages practices that run counter to the aims of providing investors with accurate information. The current direction we are taking will be what I like to call, "tell it like it is" accounting. This means an increasing reliance on fair values, when these values can be determined accurately. Financial results therefore may become more volatile. However, hiding the truth from investors will only make the shocks that markets receive more severe.
>
> The implication of this transformation in accounting is great. Assets and liabilities, when obligations exist, will be brought back on the balance sheet. The last 20 years have seen a number of attempts by companies to remove assets and liabilities from balance sheets through transactions that may obscure the economic substance of the company's financial position. This is particularly the case in four areas that warrant mention, each of which has the potential to hide the extent of a company's financial position. Companies can use all or any of the following: leases, securitizations, unconsolidated entities (special purpose entities), and pensions. These all represent legitimate operating practices, but it is also the case that in most cases the risk entailed is not recognized fully on the balance sheet of the company. When an obligation then must be met, investors can be caught by surprise.

The IASB's "*Conceptual Framework for Financial Reporting*" explains that

> [...] information about a reporting entity's financial performance helps users to understand the return that the entity has produced on its economic resources. Information about the return the entity has produced provides an indication of how well management has discharged its responsibilities to make efficient and effective use of the reporting entity's resources. Information about the variability and components of that return also is important, especially in assessing the uncertainty of future cash flows. Information about a reporting entity's past financial performance and how its management discharged its responsibilities usually is helpful in predicting the entity's future returns on its economic resources (IASB OB 16).

Moreover, the Framework states that

> [...] information about a reporting entity's financial performance during a period, reflected by changes in its economic resources and claims other than by obtaining additional resources directly from investors and creditors, is useful in assessing the entity's past and future ability to generate net cash inflows. That information indicates the extent to which the reporting entity has increased its available economic resources, and thus its capacity for generating net cash inflows through its operations rather than by obtaining additional resources directly from investors and creditors (IASB OB 18).
>
> Information about a reporting entity's financial performance during a period also may indicate the extent to which events such as changes in market prices or interest rates have increased or decreased the entity's economic resources and claims, thereby affecting the entity's ability to generate net cash inflows (IASB OB 19).
>
> Information about a reporting entity's cash flows during a period also helps users to assess the entity's ability to generate future net cash inflows. It indicates how the reporting entity obtains and spends cash, including information about its borrowing and repayment of debt, cash dividends or other cash distributions to investors, and other factors that may affect the entity's liquidity or solvency. Information about cash flows helps users understand a reporting entity's operations, evaluate its financing and investing activities, assess its liquidity or solvency, and interpret other information about financial performance (IASB OB 20).

In order to meet such commitments, the IASB requires a fuller disclosure than the European Directives. The IASB has in fact adopted the approach of forcing to write and explain everything or, as Mr. Tweede stated, "to tell it like it is". The entire liability, for instance, has to be on the balance sheet; all the companies controlled, even when they carry out different activities, have to be fitted within the consolidated area and have to be consolidated line by line; assets must or can be written at their fair value, when this value can be determined accurately. As a result, while domestic GAAP are characterized by income smoothing through its delayed and gradual recognition, IAS/IFRS are likely to reflect the effects of economic events in a more timely, even though volatile, manner.

The choice of fair value accounting by the IASB must also be considered in this perspective. Fair value accounting is expected to provide investors with useful information to predict the capacity of firms to generate cash flow from the existing resource base. Fair value should therefore play a key role in reducing the informative asymmetry between firms and investors, thus leading to a lower cost of capital for firms.

By adopting fair value accounting, the concept of income changes from income produced to mixed income, which also includes potential revenues. The concept of net capital is divested of its strictly juridical connotation and takes a more economic meaning. The introduction of fair value in fact makes net capital converge toward its market value.

Fuller accounting policies and explanatory notes are also expected to play a key role in reducing information asymmetries and improving firm value. For instance, IAS 36 "Impairment of assets" includes, among the information to be provided for each class of assets, the amount of impairment losses recognised or reversed, the recoverable amounts, the values in use and the discounting rate used in their estimation. In any case, financial statement users have to be provided with information concerning the evaluation models being used, which are otherwise handled within the company and kept strictly confidential. IAS 37 "Provisions, Contingent Liabilities and Contingent Assets" requires detailed information about contingent liabilities such as the estimate of their financial effects as well as the uncertainties about the amount or timing of the resulting outflows. The disclosure required by IFRS 7 "Financial instruments: disclosures" with regard to the financial instruments appears to be even more detailed. It consists of a considerable supply of information which ranges from basic issues such as the amount, the nature and general conditions of each financial instrument, up to information fair value and on risk management policies, especially with regard to interest rate and credit risk. IAS 14 "Segment reporting" establishes principles for reporting financial information by segment, i.e. information about the different types of products and services a firm produces and the different areas in which it operates. The explicit objectives of such detailed information are, once more, "to help users of financial statements to better understand the firm's past performance, to better assess its risk and returns and make more informed judgements about the firm as a whole" (IAS 14). As a consequence, part of the information previously used exclusively for management control purposes must now be given to the market in order to reduce information asymmetries.

3. The IAS/IFRS endorsement process in the European Union

With the adoption of IAS/IFRS for (at least) all listed firms, the European Union has in substance delegated the development of accounting standards to an international private standard setter over which it has no control. This is a remarkable move because it contrasts with the previous pattern of accounting standard setting, whose domain was that of political interest groups that did not want to lose influence. As outlined by Benston *et al.* (2006), a loss of control of accounting standard setting seems unavoidable if internationally developed standards are desired. Nevertheless, many critics were concerned about the loss of power of setting accounting standards and also questioned whether the delegation of standard setting to the IASB was lawful under the European Union's Treaties.

To address these concerns, Regulation 1606/2002 contains an endorsement mechanism that would guarantee that IAS/IFRS are adopted only provided that they conform with the "true and fair view" that is dominant in the European Directives, they are conducive to the European public good (which is not however elaborated on), and they meet the criteria of understandability, relevance, reliability, and comparability. All the IAS/IFRS must be evaluated along these lines before they are endorsed. Art. 3 of Regulation 1606/2002 states in fact that

> [...] the Commission shall decide on the applicability within the Community of international accounting standards. The international accounting standards can only be adopted if they are not contrary to the principle set out in Article 2(3) of Directive 78/660/EEC and in Article 16(3) of Directive 83/349/EEC and are conducive to the European public good and they meet the criteria of understandability, relevance, reliability and comparability required of the financial information needed for making economic decisions and assessing the stewardship of management.

The endorsement process involves many institutions and committees at the European level. Figure 1 describes the IAS/IFRS endorsement process in the European Union.

Figure 1: The IAS/IFRS endorsement process in the European Union.

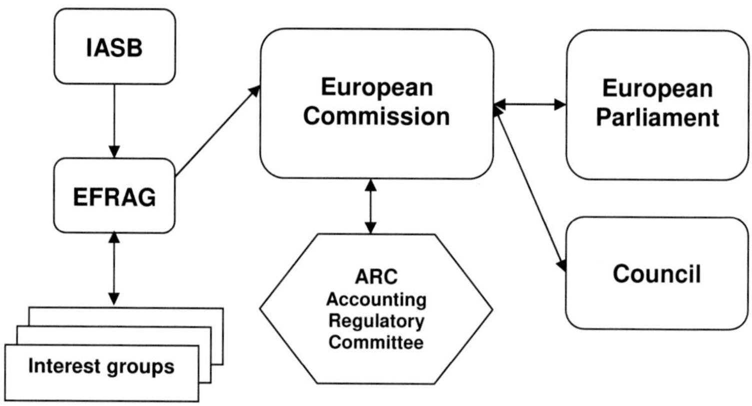

The IASB (The International Accounting Standards Board) issues a standard.

The European Financial Advisory Group (EFRAG) and the Accounting Regulatory Committee (ARC) have been established to help the Commission make the endorsement decision. EFRAG is a technical expert committee designed to provide technical assessment of IAS/IFRS in the European context and contribute to the work of the IASB on a proactive basis.

EFRAG holds consultations with interest groups and then delivers its advice to the Commission on whether the standard meets the criteria of endorsement. EFRAG also prepares in cooperation with the Commission a study on the potential economic effects of a given standard's application in the European Union.

Based on the advice of EFRAG, the Commission prepares a draft endorsement Regulation. The adoption of the Regulation follows a regulatory comitology procedure with scrutiny. First of all, ARC votes on the Commission proposal. ARC is composed of representatives from member states, hence it represents the political level in the endorsement process. It makes decisions on a qualified majority rule.

If the ARC's vote is favourable, which is the case for the vast majority of the standards to be endorsed, the European Parliament and the Council of the European Union have 3 months to oppose the adoption of the draft Regulation by the Commission. If the European Parliament and the Council give their favourable opinion on the adoption or the 3 months elapse without opposition from their side, the Commission adopts the draft Regulation. After adoption, it is published in the Official Journal and enters into force on the day defined in the Regulation itself.

4. The effects of the IAS/IFRS adoption on accounting quality

As discussed above, previous research has documented the persistence of a wide range of cross-country differences in domestic accounting standards under the Fourth and Seventh Directives. An additional attempt at integration has therefore been represented by the European Union Regulation No. 1606/2002, which has mandated IAS/IFRS for all European companies listed on European markets from 2005 onwards.

According to Regulation 1606/2002, the IAS/IFRS adoption should ensure a high degree of transparency in financial reporting.

Several studies have provided early evidence supporting this expectation. Barth *et al.* (2008), for instance, compare domestic standards and IAS/IFRS across 21 countries and document that firms applying IAS/IFRS exhibit less earnings management, more timely loss recognition, and more value relevant accounting measures. Similar results are reported by Bartov *et al.* (2005) and Gassen and Sellhorn (2006) for a single country: Germany. Bartov *et al.*

(2005) show that IAS/IFRS earnings are more value relevant than domestic GAAP, while Gassen and Sellhorn (2006) find that IAS/IFRS earnings are more persistent and conditionally conservative.

Ashbaugh and Pincus (2001) also document a reduction in analysts' forecast errors after the IAS/IFRS adoption, which is attributed to IAS/IFRS providing more predictable measures. Along the same line, Daske and Gebhardt (2006) show an increase in disclosure quality under IAS/IFRS in Austria, Germany, and Switzerland in the period prior to the mandatory adoption in 2005.

When interpreting the results of the above-mentioned studies it must, however, be taken into account that they refer to voluntary adoption of IAS/IFRS, which might be the result of corporate incentives to increase transparency.

Ashbaugh (2001), for instance, documents that the decision to report under IAS/IFRS is positively related to corporate size, the number of foreign equity markets on which the firm's shares are traded, and the additional issuance of equity shares. Similar findings are reported by Cuijpers and Buijink (2005) and Gassen and Sellhorn (2006). For a sample of European non-financial firms voluntarily adopting IAS/IFRS, Cuijpers and Buijink (2005) document that foreign listing and geographical dispersion of operations are important drivers. Gassen and Sellhorn (2006) also show that size, international exposure, dispersion of ownership and IPOs are important determinants of voluntary IAS/IFRS adoption by publicly traded German firms.

Overall, these studies suggest that companies voluntarily shifting to IAS/IFRS have had incentives to improve transparency and the quality of financial reporting. Along the same line, Covrig, Defond, and Hung (2007) document that foreign mutual fund ownership is significantly higher among IAS/IFRS adopters, which suggest a voluntary switch to IAS/IFRS aimed at attracting foreign investors by providing them with both more information and information that is more familiar to them.

Since the same incentives are not likely to be found when IAS/IFRS adoption is mandatory, results referring to voluntary shifts may not extrapolate to mandatory adoption cases. Christensen *et al.* (2008), for instance, provide evidence consistent with this view. They investigate voluntary and mandatory shifts to IAS/IFRS in Germany, where firms were allowed to switch to IAS/IFRS prior to 2005, and find that voluntary adoption is associated with an increase in accounting quality, whereas such an improvement is not observed in the case of mandatory shifts. Their findings therefore suggest that high quality accounting standards such as IAS/IFRS do not necessarily lead to higher quality accounting, at least when firms do not perceive net benefits from IAS/IFRS adoption.

This evidence is in line with Daske *et al.* (2012) who also find that changes in firms' reporting incentives play a significant role in the commitment to increased disclosure for firms voluntarily adopting IAS/IFRS. Daske *et al.* consider differences between entities which are "serious" IAS/IFRS adopters versus those which only seek to use the IAS/IFRS "label", where seriousness is defined in terms of commitment to financial reporting transparency. They find that serious adopters experience significantly stronger, i. e. favourable, effects on the cost of capital and market liquidity than label adopters.

Such findings have brought many researchers and observers to the conclusion that the IAS/IFRS adoption *per se* would not necessarily improve financial reporting and to question the effectiveness of the mandatory IAS/IFRS adoption on financial reporting quality.

The IAS/IFRS adoption by European companies required by Regulation 1606/2002 has therefore represented an extraordinary event for empirical research, which could investigate the effects of the mandatory IAS/IFRS adoption in Europe.

Early evidence on stock market perception of the economic consequences of the IAS/IFRS mandatory adoption in Europe shows that equity investors perceived the benefits of their adoption.

Comprix *et al.* (2003), for instance, identify 11 dates between 2000 and 2002 that signal the likelihood or the timing of the IAS/IFRS adoption in the European Union and find that the stock market reacted positively to news that increased the likelihood of the IAS/IFRS adoption. Armstrong *et al.* (2010) also investigate the European stock market reactions to 16 events associated with the adoption of IAS/IFRS in Europe, such as the European Parliament Resolution requiring all EU listed companies to use IAS/IFRS, or the endorsement of all IAS/IFRS except for IAS 32 and 39, or the IAS 39 endorsement with carved out provisions. They find that the stock market reaction was significantly positive (negative) in reaction to events that increased (decreased) the likelihood of the adoption, and that the reaction was stronger for firms that did not cross-list in the United States.

In contrast to the three-day window test in Armstrong *et al.*, Pae *et al.* (2008) focus on the reduction of Tobin's Q associated with agency costs in a long-window test over the period when the European Union moved to IAS/IFRS. They find that from 1999 to 2003 Tobin's Q increased more for European firms that were not listed in the United States, were family-controlled and had low analyst following. Pae *et al.* attribute these findings to the announcements of IAS/IFRS adoption in the European Union, which lead to expectations of reduced future agency costs.

Several studies have focused on the effects of mandating IAS/IFRS in different countries contemporarily.

Aubert and Grudnitski (2011), for instance, investigate the IAS/IFRS impact on the European Union by considering 13 countries and 20 industries at the same time, but fail to document a statistically significant increase in the value relevance of accounting information after the IAS/IFRS adoption.

Other studies have highlighted the role of the firm environment in determining the impact of mandatory IAS/IFRS adoption. Daske *et al.* (2008), for instance, examine the mandatory IAS/IFRS adoption not only in Europe, but worldwide. They analyse the effects of adopting IAS/IFRS in 26 countries on market liquidity, cost of capital and Tobin's Q and find an increase in market liquidity around the time of the IAS/IFRS adoption. They also document a decrease in firms' cost of equity and an increase in equity valuation, but only if prior effects to the adoption date are accounted for. Taken as a whole, their evidence suggests modest, but economically significant capital market benefits around the IAS/IFRS mandatory adoption. Such market benefits occurred, however, only in countries where firms had incentives to be transparent and where legal enforcement was strong, thus suggesting that enforcement regimes and firms' reporting incentives play a major role in capital market benefits from the IAS/IFRS adoption. In the other countries, market liquidity and value instead remained largely unchanged in the year of the mandatory adoption.

In addition, capital market effects of the IAS/IFRS adoption were larger for firms in countries with domestic standards of lower quality and differing more from IAS/IFRS.

Aharony *et al.* (2010) compare the value relevance of accounting information in 14 European countries in the year prior to and the year of the mandatory adoption of the IAS/IFRS. They focus on three accounting information items for which measurements under IAS/IFRS are likely to differ considerably from measurements under domestic GAAP: goodwill, research and development expenses (R&D), and asset revaluation. By using valuation models that include these three variables in addition to book value of equity and earnings, Aharony *et al.* show that adopting IAS/IFRS increases their value relevance to investors. They also report additional evidence of cross-country differences in the incremental value relevance of IAS/IFRS as investors benefited most from implementing IAS/IFRS for such items in the European Union countries where local standards deviated more from IAS/IFRS.

These results are in line with Byard *et al.* (2011) and Horton *et al.* (2012), who also document the important roles of enforcement regimes and firm-level reporting incentives in determining the impact of mandatory IAS/IFRS adoption. Byard *et al.* (2011) report a decrease in analysts' absolute forecast errors and forecast dispersion, relative to a control sample which voluntarily adopted IAS/IFRS at least two years prior to the mandatory adoption date, only for those mandatory adopters domiciled in countries with both strong enforcement regimes and domestic accounting standards that differ significantly from IAS/IFRS. Furthermore, for mandatory adopters domiciled in countries with both weak enforcement regimes and domestic accounting standards that differ significantly from IAS/IFRS, they find that forecast errors and dispersion decreased more for firms with stronger incentives for transparent financial reporting. Horton *et al.* (2012) also find that after the mandatory IAS/IFRS adoption, consensus forecast errors decreased for firms that mandatorily adopted IAS/IFRS relative to forecast errors of other firms, even though the magnitude of the forecast errors was associated with firm-specific differences between domestic GAAP and IAS/IFRS.

Beuselinck *et al.* (2010) also find that the mandatory IAS/IFRS adoption had a significant and positive effect on information processing by financial analysts, but this did not occur homogeneously across them. Beuselinck *et al.* examine whether the mandatory IAS/IFRS adoption in Europe reduced firm opacity and contributed to stock price informativeness. Their findings document a V-shaped pattern in stock return synchronicity around IAS/IFRS adoption, which is consistent with IAS/IFRS disclosures revealing new firm-specific information in the adoption period (i.e. a reduction of synchronicity) and subsequently lowering the surprise of future disclosures (i.e. an increase in synchronicity). Furthermore, findings show that the mandatory IAS/IFRS adoption increased analyst ability to incorporate industry-level information into stock prices and reduced private information advantage enjoyed by institutional owners. These effects were, however, driven by firms domiciled in strong enforcement countries, which suggests the importance of enforcement quality for the transparency effects of IAS/IFRS.

Likewise, Barth *et al.* (2012) report that the adjustments to net income resulting from the mandatory IAS/IFRS adoption in Europe are value relevant, even though such value relevance is affected by differences in institutional factors or domestic standards. Kvaal and Nobes (2010) find significant evidence that pre-IAS/IFRS national practices continue where this is allowed within IAS/IFRS, thus documenting the existence of national patterns of accounting within IAS/IFRS.

Finally, Macias and Muiño (2011) document that countries requiring the use of local standards in separate financial statements exhibit a significantly lower level of accounting quality, both prior to and following the IFRS adoption, which suggests that these countries have domestic standards more oriented towards the satisfaction of regulatory needs rather than towards those of investors.

Taken as a whole, these studies suggest that if, on the one hand, there are arguments to support an improvement in accounting quality under IAS/IFRS, on the other hand, there are also reasons to think that mandatory adoption by itself is not sufficient to increase the quality of financial reporting.

Some studies have investigated the mandatory IAS/IFRS adoption in individual countries, with the important advantage of reducing the omitted variables problem. These studies have however provided controversial results. Some of them find that IAS/IFRS are more value relevant than domestic GAAP, others find them to be otherwise, still others find no significant difference between IAS/IFRS and domestic GAAP. As discussed hereafter, such mixed results can be attributable to different levels of legal enforcement and firm incentives in adopting IAS/IFRS.

Callao *et al.* (2007), for instance, examine the effect of adopting IAS/IFRS on the usefulness of financial reporting in Spain by looking at two of the key characteristics of usefulness, comparability and value relevance of financial reporting. They test for differences in financial figures and ratios calculated under both domestic GAAP and IFRS and find that value relevance of financial reporting did not improve, whereas comparability even worsened after the IAS/IFRS implementation.

Along the same line, Navarro–Garcia and Bastida (2010) surveyed the financial statement preparers of Spanish listed firms to determine their perception of the appropriateness of IAS/IFRS for decision making. Their results confirm those of Callao *et al.*, that is, IAS/IFRS are not considered to be more appropriate than Spanish accounting standards. IAS/IFRS are perceived to be of high quality, but complex and too flexible. In addition, costs of compliance with the new standards outweigh the perceived benefits, including enhanced international comparisons.

Horton and Serafeim (2010) examine the market reaction to and the value relevance of IAS/IFRS reconciliation forms for firms listed on the UK stock market. Findings show that consensus forecast errors are lower for firms that mandatorily adopted IFRS compared to forecast errors of other firms and that the improvement in the information environment is driven both by information and comparability effects. Christensen *et al.* (2007) investigate a similar setting, but focus on the effect of the IAS/IFRS adoption on debt contracting. Using abnormal returns, they find significant market reactions to IAS/IFRS reconciliation announcements, which are more pronounced among firms facing greater likelihood and costs of covenant violation. They also show that market reactions to reconciliation forms are weaker for later announcements, consistently with the contractual implication of technical changes to earnings which investors quickly learn to predict.

Gjerde *et al.* (2008) focus on IAS/IFRS restatements for firms listed on the Oslo Stock Exchange and find mixed results. On the one hand, their analysis provides little evidence of increased value relevance for IAS/IFRS numbers when comparing and evaluating the two accounting sets unconditionally. On the other hand, when evaluating the change in accounting figures, the reconciliation adjustments are IAS/IFRS marginally value relevant.

Iatridis and Rouvolis (2010) evaluate the value relevance of IAS/IFRS financial statements for Greek listed firms documenting that IFRS-based financial statement measures have higher value relevance than those prepared under Greek GAAP. Their study also determines that firm size and level of financing are positively associated with the provision of voluntary disclosures.

Zeghal *et al.* (2012) focus on French companies and find that the mandatory IAS/IFRS adoption is associated with a reduction in the earnings management level. Moreover, the independence and the efficiency of the board of directors, the existence of an independent audit committee, the existence of block shareholders, the quality of the external audit and the listing on foreign financial markets are important factors for IAS/IFRS enforcement. In fact, the mandatory adoption of IAS/IFRS decreases the earnings management level especially for companies with good corporate governance and those depending on foreign financial markets.

Barth *et al.* (2008) argue that one explanation for such mixed findings in individual country research is that firms adopting IAS/IFRS most likely transitioned gradually, modifying accounting amounts based on domestic standards in order to be closer to those based on IAS/IFRS. For example, Hung and Subramanyan (2007) find few reconciling items related to earnings management, such as hidden reserves, which is surprising because the existence of such earnings management items has always been a common concern with the application of German standards.

Clarkson *et al.* (2011) also highlight that some of the mixed results could be driven by methodological issues, such as measurement errors introduced by accounting standards.

Another explanation is that these studies differ in the effectiveness of controls for incentives associated with a firm's use of a particular set of accounting standards and effects of the economic environment. Several studies have in fact shown that enforcement regimes and firms' reporting incentives play a major role for capital market benefits from the IAS/IFRS adoption. As discussed above, Daske *et al.* (2008), Beuselinck *et al.* (2010), Aharoni *et al.* (2010), Kvaal and Nobes (2010), Byard *et al.* (2011), Barth *et al.* (2012) and Horton *et al.* (2012) show that accounting quality under IAS/IFRS differs according to the enforcement regime. Atanassova (2008) and Verriest (2010) also find that disclosure under IAS/IFRS is of higher quality when firms have strong corporate governance, thus showing that the firm-level corporate governance context can be an important determinant of financial reporting quality.

As outlined by Soderstrom and Sun (2007), research shows that, in general, accounting quality after the IAS/IFRS adoption is the result of three factors: the quality of accounting standards, the country's legal and political system, and financial reporting incentives which, in turn, are actually driven by financial market development, capital structure, ownership structure and tax system.

5. The effects of the IAS/IFRS adoption on comparability of financial reporting

Comparability, together with relevance and reliability is a key qualitative characteristic of accounting information. Comparable financial statements are believed to facilitate investors' resource allocation and investment decisions.

As mentioned, the explicit purpose of Regulation 1606/2002 mandating IAS/IFRS in the European Union is to ensure a high degree of transparency and comparability of financial statements and, hence, an efficient functioning of capital markets. According to this regulation, the adoption of IAS/IFRS within the community should provide not only a high degree of transparency of financial statements *per se*, but also a high degree of comparability of financial statements among different countries previously using different accounting standards. In this sense, accounting standardization is expected to reduce possible errors in the market evaluation of European companies due to different accounting systems. The adoption of the same accounting standard set within the European Union should improve comparability and, in this way, eliminate accounting measurement errors in pricing firms.

On the one hand, extant research has documented that spontaneous harmonization within European "global players" was already in process before the mandatory IAS/IFRS adoption. Companies competing in international markets had in fact entered a process of harmonization since the 1980s (Thorell and Whittington, 1994, Cañibano and Mora, 2000) independently of the formal political process. Land and Lang (2003), for instance, document an increase in comparability over time of accounting data of firms from Australia, Canada, France, Germany, Japan, the United Kingdom, and the United States.

On the other hand, research has pointed out that full convergence in accounting is difficult to achieve, due to a number of both firm-specific and country-specific factors (Jaafar and McLeay, 2007). Several studies have in fact shown that accounting quality depends not only on accounting standards, but also on firms' incentives to issue high-quality financial statements and on the level of legal enforcement.

The IAS/IFRS adoption in Europe has eliminated cross-country differences in one of these elements, that is, accounting standards. In the preparation of their consolidated financial statements, European listed companies apply the same set of accounting standards. However, the same degree of uniformity does not exist regarding countries' institutional frameworks and, as a consequence, regarding firms' incentives to issue high-quality financial reporting. Extant research has in fact provided evidence on the differences between European countries in their level of protection of shareholders' rights, the strength of the system of legal enforcement, the level of ownership concentration, the degree of financial and tax alignment, or the importance of the equity market (e.g., Hung, 2001; La Porta *et al.* 2006, La Porta *et al.* 1998). Moreover, it has documented the key role played by these institutional characteristics in shaping accounting quality (e.g., Ali and Hwang, 2000; Ball, Kothari, and Robin, 2000; Burgstahler, Hail, and Leuz, 2006; Bushman and Piotroski, 2006).

An attempt to investigate the capital market consequences of the IAS/IFRS adoption in terms of financial statement comparability has been carried out by DeFond *et al.* (2011). The idea behind their work is that if IAS/IFRS increase comparability and reduce the cost of comparing financial statements prepared under different GAAP, this should positively affect US mutual fund holdings in foreign firms. DeFond *et al.* use two input-based measures that look at the accounting standards adopted: the "GAAP heterogeneity measure", which captures the decrease in accounting standard heterogeneity in a given industry as a result of IAS/IFRS adoption, and the "GAAP peer measure", which is computed as the ratio of the number of firms in a given industry using IAS/IFRS subsequent to their adoption to the number of firms in the same industry applying local GAAP prior to IAS/IFRS introduction. The authors find that the benefit of increased comparability, in terms of size of mutual fund investments, is higher for voluntary than for mandatory adopters. Furthermore, for the latter, discernible effects of improved comparability only obtain in countries with serious implementation processes.

Horton *et al.* (2012) find that consensus forecast errors decrease for firms that mandatorily adopt IAS/IFRS and that the improvement in the information environment is driven both by information and comparability effects. They also show that the magnitude of the forecast errors decrease is associated with firm-specific differences between domestic GAAP and IFRS.

Using a sample of 17 European countries and three proxies to measure comparability (i.e., the similarity of accounting functions that translate economic events into accounting data, the degree of information transfer, and the similarity of the information content of earnings and book value), Yip and Young (2012) also provide evidence of increased accounting comparability following IAS/IFRS adoption.

Based on a sample of UK firms, which already had domestic standards similar to IAS/IFRS, Brochet *et al.* (2012) document a decrease in information asymmetries, as measured by abnormal returns, following the introduction of IAS/IFRS. They link this positive capital market consequence to firm-level changes in comparability and interpret it as evidence for an increase in accounting comparability. Likewise, Wang (2011) finds that mandatory adopters experience a significant increase in market reactions to earnings announcements compared to pre-mandatory adoption. Since this increase is not observed for non-adopters, they interpret it as indicative of IAS/IFRS increasing comparability.

Liao *et al.* (2012) focus on cross-country comparability of IAS/IFRS financial reporting by investigating the valuation usefulness of earnings and book values in France and Germany after the IAS/IFRS mandatory adoption. To assess comparability they use accounting-based valuation models as under the efficient hypothesis that a dollar of reported book value and earning should be priced equivalently by investors if the accounting measure reflects the same underlying economic value. Their study focuses on France and Germany because they represent the European Union's major economies and largest capital markets, suggesting therefore efficient equity markets. Moreover, they have similar social-economic institutions, which, as prior research indicates, affect a firm's accounting measures (Alford *et al.* 1993, Ball *et al.* 2000). Findings document that French and German IAS/IFRS earnings and book values are comparable in the year subsequent to IAS/IFRS adoption, but become less comparable in the years that follow as over time managers tend to implement IAS/IFRS differently.

De Franco *et al.* (2011) propose a measure of financial statement comparability which reflects the idea that, if the same economic events are accounted for homogeneously by two firms, the two firms should have comparable accounting systems. Empirically, the authors proxy for economic events and the output of financial statements using stock returns and earnings, respectively: the more similar the mapping between earnings and returns across firms, the more comparable the accounting systems. Findings show that their measure is positively related to analyst following and forecast accuracy and negatively related to analysts' dispersion in earnings forecasts, which suggests that financial statement comparability lowers the cost of acquiring information and increases the overall quantity and quality of information available to analysts.

Several studies have used measures based on de Franco *et al.* in order to test the effect of the mandatory IAS/IFRS adoption on comparability (Lang *et al.* 2010, André *et al.* 2012, Barth *et al.* 2012, Cascino and Gassen 2012). These studies have provided mixed results, but all have suggested that, as seen for accounting quality, the effect of mandatory IAS/IFRS adoption on financial statement comparability is affected by legal enforcement and firm incentives.

Cascino and Gassen (2012), for instance, have focused on cross-country comparability and find that the overall effect of mandating IAS/IFRS is marginal. Findings show in fact that firm-, region-, and country-level incentives systematically shape accounting compliance and that only firms with high compliance incentives experience substantial increases in comparability. Likewise, Lang *et al.* (2010) examine comparability in a cross-country setting, with many country-level legal and institutional control variables, and find that the mandatory adoption of IAS/IFRS increases earnings comovement, but does not increase true cross-country comparability.

André *et al.* (2012) focus on cross-industry comparability and find significant convergence in firms' accounting practices in Europe following the IAS/IFRS adoption, even though comparability do not improve with IAS/IFRS familiarity. Furthermore, they find that analysts' forecasts errors decline as comparability increases, thus suggesting that comparability increases the usefulness of accounting information and facilitates investors in valuing firms more accurately.

Barth *et al.* (2012) investigate, instead, whether the adoption of IAS/IFRS by non-US firms increases the comparability of accounting information with respect to US firms applying US GAAP and find that, after the IAS/IFRS adoption, IAS/IFRS and US GAAP firms exhibited higher value relevance comparability, although some differences still persisted.

Finally, Kim *et al.* (2012) develop an empirical measure of comparability, designed to capture comparability benefits from the perspective of debt holders, based on the within-industry variability of Moody's adjustments to firms' reported accounting numbers, and report benefits of comparability to debt market participants.

In conclusion, the literature on the effects of the mandatory IAS/IFRS adoption on comparability has shown that the switch to IAS/IFRS is not a condition *per se* to improve comparability across firms as legal enforcement and firm incentives play a key role. Therefore, as accounting quality is a function of the firms' overall institutional settings, including the legal and the political system of the country in which firms reside, cross-country differences in accounting quality are likely to remain even after accounting standardization through the IAS/IFRS adoption in all the European countries.

References

Aharony, J., R. Barniv and H. Falk (2010), "The impact of mandatory IFRS adoption on equity valuation of accounting numbers for security investors in the EU", *The European Accounting Review,* 19(3), 535–578.

Alford, A., J. Jones, R. Leftwitch and M. Zmijeski (1993), "The relative informativeness of accounting disclosure in different countries", *Journal of Accounting Research,* 31, Supplement, 183–223.

Ali, A. and L. S. Hwang (2000), "Country-specific factors related to financial reporting and value relevance of accounting data", *Journal of Accounting Research,* 38, 1–21.

André, P., D. Dionysiou and I. Tsalavoutas (2012), *Mandatory adoption of IFRS by EU listed firms and comparability : determinants and analysts forecasts.* Working paper, Essec Business School.

Armstrong, C., M. Barth, A. Jagolinzer and E. Riedl (2010), "Market reaction to the adoption of IFRS in Europe", *The Accounting Review,* 85(1), 31–61.

Ashbaugh, H. (2001), "Non-US firms' accounting standard choices", *Journal of Accounting and Public Policy,* 20, 129–153.

Ashbaugh, H. and M. Pincus (2001), "Domestic accounting standards, International Accounting Standards, and the predictability of earnings", *Journal of Accounting Research,* 39, 417–434.

Ashbaugh, H. and P. Olsson (2002), "An exploratory study of the valuation properties of crosslisted firms' IAS and U.S. GAAP earnings and book values", *The Accounting Review,* 77, 107–126.

Atanassova, A. (2008), *IFRS-adoption in Bulgarian banks: non-numerical disclosure evidence.* INTACCT Working paper, University of Economics, Varna.

Aubert, F. and G. Grudnitski (2011), "The impact and importance of mandatory adoption of International Financial Reporting Standards in Europe", *Journal of International Financial Management & Accounting,* 22(1), 1–26.

Ball, R., S. P. Kothari and A. Robin (2000), "The effect of international institutional factors on properties of accounting earnings", *Journal of Accounting and Economics,* 29, 1–51.

Ball, R. (2001), "Infrastructure requirements for an economically efficient system of public financial reporting and disclosure", *Brookings-Wharton Papers on Financial Service,* 127–169.

Ball, R., A. Robin and J. Wu (2003), "Incentives versus standards: properties of accounting income in four East Asian countries", *Journal of Accounting and Economic,* 36, 235–270.

Ball, R. and L. Shivakumar (2005), "Earnings quality in U.K. private firms", *Journal of Accounting and Economics,* 39, 83–128.

Ball, R. (2006), "IFRS: Pros and cons for investors", *Accounting and Business Research,* International Accounting Policy Forum, 5–27.

Barth, M. (2008), "Global financial reporting: Implications for U.S. academics", *The Accounting Review,* 83, 1159–1179.

Barth, M., W. Landsman and M. Lang (2008), "International Accounting Standards and accounting quality", *Journal of Accounting Research,* 46, 467–498.

Barth, M., W. Landsman, D. Young and Z. Zhuang (2011), *Relevance of differences between net income based on IFRS and domestic standards for European firms.* Working paper, Stanford University, University of North Carolina, and Chinese University of Hong Kong.

Barth, M., W. Landsman, M. Lang and C. Williams (2012), "Are IFRS based and US GAAP-based accounting amounts comparable?", *Journal of Accounting and Economics,* 54(1), 68–93.

Barth, M., W. Landsman, M. Lang and C. Williams (2012), "Are International Accounting Standards-based and US GAAP-based accounting amounts comparable?", *Journal of Accounting and Economics,* forthcoming.

Bartov, E., S. Goldberg and M. Kim (2005), "Comparative value relevance among German, U.S. and International Accounting Standards: A German stock market perspective", *Journal of Accounting, Auditing and Finance,* 20, 95–119.

Baruch S., G.A. Karolyi and M. Lemmon (2007), "Multi-market trading and liquidity: Theory and evidence", *The Journal of Finance,* 62, 2169–2200.

Benston, G.J., M. Bromwich, R.E. Litan and A. Wagenhofer (2006), *Worlwide financial reporting. The development and future of accounting standards,* Oxford, Oxford University Press.

Beuselinck, C., P. Joos, I. Khurana and S. Van der Meulen (2010), *Mandatory IFRS reporting and stock price informativeness.* Working paper, Tilburg University and University of Missouri at Columbia.

Botosan, C. and M. Plumlee (2005), "Assessing alternative proxies for the expected risk premium", *The Accounting Review,* 80, 21–53.

Bradshaw, M., S. Richardson and R. Sloan (2001), "Do analysts and auditors use information in accruals?", *Journal of Accounting Research,* 39, 45–74.

Bradshaw, M. and G. Miller (2008), "Will harmonizing accounting standards really harmonize accounting? Evidence from non-U.S. firms adopting U.S. GAAP", *Journal of Accounting, Auditing and Finance,* 23, 233–264.

Brennan, M. and A. Subrahmanyam (1996), "Market microstructure and asset pricing: On the compensation for illiquidity in stock returns", *Journal of Financial Economics,* 41, 441–464.

Brochet, F., A. Jagolinzer and E.J. Riedl (2012), "Mandatory IFRS adoption and financial statement comparability", *Contemporary Accounting Research,* Forthcoming.
Burgstahler, D., L. Hail and C. Leuz (2006), "The importance of reporting incentives: Earnings management in European private and public firms", *The Accounting Review,* 81, 983–1017.
Bushman, R.M. and J.D. Piotroski (2006), "Financial reporting incentives for conservative accounting: The influence of legal and political institutions", *Journal of Accounting and Economics*, 42, 107–148.
Bushman, R. and W.R. Landsman (2010), "The pros and cons of regulating corporate reporting: a critical review of the arguments", *Accounting and Business Research,* 40(3), 259–273.
Byard, D., Y. Li and Y. Yu (2011), "The effect of mandatory IFRS adoption on financial analysts' information environment", *Journal of Accounting Research,* 49(1), 69–96.
Cairns, D. (1999), *International Accounting Standards Survey*, LLP Professional Publishing.
Cairns, D. (2000), *International Accounting Standards Survey.*
Callao, S., J.I. Jarne and J.A. Lainez (2007), "Adoption of IFRS in Spain: effect on the comparability and relevance of financial reporting", *Journal of International Accounting, Auditing and Taxation*, 16, 148–178.
Callao, S. and J.I. Jarne (2010), "Have IFRS affected earnings management in the European Union?", *Accounting in Europe,* 7(2), 159–189.
Cañibano, L. and A. Mora (2000), "Evaluating the statistical significance of de facto accounting harmonization: A study of European global players", *European Accounting Review*, 9(3), 349–369.
Cascino, S. and J. Gassen (2012), *What Drives the comparability effect of mandatory IFRS adoption?.* Working paper.
Christensen, H., E. Lee and M. Walker (2007), "Cross-sectional variation in the economic consequences of international accounting harmonization: The case of mandatory IFRS adoption in the UK", *International Journal of Accounting,* 42, 341–379.
Christensen, H.B., E. Lee and M. Walker (2008), "Incentives or standards: What determines accounting quality changes around IFRS adoption?". Working paper.
Chua, W. and S. Taylor (2008), "The rise and rise of IFRS: an examination of IFRS diffusion", *Journal of Accounting and Public Policy*, 27, 462–473.
Clarkson, P., J.D. Hanna, G.D. Richardson and R. Thompson (2011), "The impact of IFRS adoption on the value relevance of book value and earnings", *Journal of Contemporary Accounting and Economics*, 7(1), 1–17.
Coffee, J. (1999), "The future as history: The prospects for global convergence in corporate governance and its implications", *Northwestern University Law Review,* 93, 641–708.
Comprix, J., K. Muller and M. Stanford (2003), *Economic consequences from mandatory adoption of IASB standards in the European Union.* Working paper.

Covrig, V., M. DeFond and M. Hung (2007), "Home bias, foreign mutual fund holdings, and the voluntary adoption of International Accounting Standards", *Journal of Accounting Research,* 45, 41–70.

Cuijpers, R. and W. Buijink (2005), "Voluntary adoption of non-local GAAP in the European Union: A study of determinants and consequences", *European Accounting Review,* 14, 487–524.

Daske, H. (2006), "Economic benefits of adopting IFRS or US-GAAP: Have the expected costs of equity capital really decreased?", *Journal of Business Finance and Accounting,* 33, 329–373.

Daske, H. and G. Gebhardt (2006), "International Financial Reporting Standards and experts' perceptions of disclosure quality", *Abacus,* 42, 461–498.

Daske, H., L. Hail, C. Leuz and R. Verdi (2008), "Mandatory IFRS reporting around the world: Early evidence on the economic consequences", *Journal of Accounting Research,* 46(5), 1085–1142.

Daske, H., L. Hail, C. Leuz and R. Verdi (2012), "Adopting a label: heterogeneity in the economic consequences around IAS/IFRS adoptions", *Journal of Accounting Research,* forthcoming.

De Franco, G., S.P. Kothari and R.S. Verdi (2011), "The Benefits of Financial Statement Comparability", *Journal of Accounting Research*, 49, 895–931.

Defond, M.L., X. Hu, M. Hung and S. Li (2011), "The impact of IFRS adoption on U.S. mutual fund ownership: The role of comparability", *Journal of Accounting and Economics,* 51, 240–258.

Ding, Y., T. Jeanjean and H. Stolowy (2005), "Why do national GAAP differ from IAS? The role of culture", *The International Journal of Accounting,* 40, 325–350.

Ding, Y., O.-K. Hope, T. Jeanjean and H. Stolowy (2007), "Differences between domestic accounting standards and IAS: Measurement, determinants and implications", *Journal of Accounting and Public Policy,* 26, 1–38.

Djankov, S., R. La Porta, F. Lopez-de-Silanes and A. Shleifer (2008), "The law and economics of self-dealing", *Journal of Financial Economics,* 88, 430–465.

Doidge, C., G.A. Karolyi and R. Stulz (2004), "Why are foreign firms listed in the U.S. worth more?", *Journal of Financial Economics,* 71, 205–238.

Eberhartinger, E. and M. Klostermann (2007), "What if IFRS were a tax base? New empirical evidence from an Austrian perspective", *Accounting in Europe*, 4(2), 141–168.

Foerster, S. and G.A. Karolyi (1999), "The effects of market segmentation and investor recognition on asset prices: Evidence from foreign stocks listing in the United States", *The Journal of Finance,* 54, 981–1013.

Gassen, J. and T. Selhorn (2006), "Applying IFRS in Germany – determinants and consequences", *Betriebswirtschaftliche Forschung und Praxis*, 58(3).

Gjerde, O., K. Knivsfla and F. Saettem (2008), "The value-relevance of adopting IFRS: evidence from 145 NGAAP restatements", *Journal of International Accounting, Auditing and Taxation*, 17, 92–112.

Hail, L. and C. Leuz (2007), "Capital market effects of mandatory IFRS reporting in the EU: empirical evidence", Report made available by the Netherlands Authority for the Financial Markets (AFM).

Hail, L., C. Leuz and P. Wysocki (2010), "Global accounting convergence and the potential adoption of IFRS by the U.S. (part I): Conceptual underpinnings and economic analysis", *Accounting Horizons,* 24(3), 355–394.

Harris, M. and K. Muller III (1999), "The market valuation of IAS versus US-GAAP accounting measures using Form 20-F reconciliations", *Journal of Accounting and Economics,* 26, 285–312.

Hodgdon, C., R. Tondkar, D. Harless and A. Adhikari (2008), "Compliance with IFRS disclosure requirements and individual analysts' forecast errors", *Journal of International Accounting, Auditing and Taxation*, 17, 1–13.

Horton, J. and G. Serafeim (2010), "Market reaction to and valuation of IFRS reconciliation adjustments: first evidence from the UK", *Review of Accounting Studies,* 15(4), 725–751.

Horton, J., G. Serafeim and I. Serafeim (2012), "Does mandatory IFRS adoption improve the information environment?", *Contemporary Accounting Research.*

Hung, M. (2001), "Accounting standards and value relevance of financial statements: An international analysis", *Journal of Accounting and Economics,* 30, 401–420.

Hung, M. and K. Subramanyam (2007), "Financial statement effects of adopting International Accounting Standards: The case of Germany", *Review of Accounting Studies,* 12, 623–657.

Iatridis, G. and S. Rouvolis (2010), "The post-adoption effects of the implementation of International Financial Reporting Standard in Greece", *Journal of International Accounting, Auditing and Taxation*, 19, 55–65.

Jaafar, A. and S. McLeay (2007), "Country effects and sector effects on the harmonization of accounting policy choice", *Abacus*, 43(2), 156–189.

Jeanjean T. and H. Stolowy (2008), "Do accounting standards matter? An explanatory analysis of earnings management before and after IFRS adoption", *Journal of Accounting Public Policy*, 27, 480–494.

Jermakowicz, E. (2004), "Effects of adoption of International Financial Reporting Standards in Belgium: the evidence from BEL-20companies", *Accounting in Europe*, 1(1), 51–70.

Jermakowicz, E. and S. Gornik-Tomaszewski (2006), "Implementing IFRS from the perspective of EU publicly traded companies", *Journal of International Accounting, Auditing and Taxation,* 15, 170–196.

Jermakowicz, E., J. Prather-Kinsey and I. Wulf (2007), "The value relevance of accounting income reported by DAX-30 German companies", *Journal of International Financial Management & Accounting*, 18, n. 3, September 2007.

Kim, S., P. Kraft and S. Ryan (2012), *Financial statement comparability and credit risk.* Working paper, New York University, Stern School of Business.

Kothari, S.P. (2001), "Capital markets research in accounting", *Journal of Accounting and Economics,* 31, 105–231.

Kothari, S.P., A. Leone and C. Wasley (2005), "Performance matched discretionary accrual measures", *Journal of Accounting and Economics,* 39, 163–197.

Kvaal, E. and C. Nobes (2010), "International differences in IFRS policy choice: a research note", *Accounting and Business Research,* 40(2), 173–187.

Kvaal, E. and C. Nobes (2012), "IFRS policy changes and the continuation of national pat-terns of IFRS practice", *The European Accounting Review*, 21(2), 343–371.

La Porta, R., F. Lopez-de-Silanes, A. Shleifer and R. Vishny (1997), "Legal determinants of external finance", *The Journal of Finance,* 52, 1131–1150.

La Porta, R., F. Lopez-de-Silanes, A. Shleifer and R.W. Vishny (1998), "Law and finance", *The Journal of Political Economy*, 106(6), 1113–1155.

La Porta, R., F. Lopez-de-Silanes and A. Shleifer (2006), "What works in securities laws?", *The Journal of Finance*, 61(1), 1–32.

Land, J. and M.H. Lang (2003), "Empirical evidence on the evolution of international earnings", *The Accounting Review*, 77, 115–133.

Landsman, W., E. Maydew and J. Thornock (2012), "The information content of annual earnings announcements and mandatory adoption of IFRS", *Journal of Accounting and Economics*, 53(1–2), 34–54.

Lang, M. and R. Lundholm (1996), "Corporate disclosure policy and analyst behaviour", *The Accounting Review,* 71, 467–492.

Lang, M., K. Lins and D. Miller (2004), "Concentrated control, analyst following, and valuation: Do analysts matter most when investors are protected least?", *Journal of Accounting Research,* 42, 589–623.

Lang, M., J. Smith Raedy and W. Wilson (2006), "Earnings management and cross listing: Are reconciled earnings comparable to US earnings?", *Journal of Accounting and Economics,* 42, 255–283.

Lang, M., M.G. Maffett and E.L. Owens (2010), *Earnings comovement and accounting comparability: The effects of mandatory IFRS adoption*. Working paper, University of Rochester.

Lang, M., K. Lins and M. Maffett (2012), "Transparency, liquidity, and valuation: International evidence on when transparency matters most", *Journal of Accounting Research*, forthcoming.

Leuz, C. and R. Verrecchia (2000), "The economic consequences of increased disclosure", *Journal of Accounting Research,* 38, 91–124.

Leuz, C. (2003), "IAS versus US GAAP: Information asymmetry-based evidence from Germany's New Market", *Journal of Accounting Research,* 41, 445–472.

Leuz, C., D. Nanda and P. Wysocki (2003), "Earnings management and investor protection: an international comparison", *Journal of Financial Economics,* 69, 505–527.

Leuz, C. (2006), "Cross listing, bonding and firms' reporting incentives: A discussion of Lang, Raedy and Wilson", *Journal of Accounting and Economics,* 42, 285–299.

Leuz, C. and P. Wysocki (2009), *Economic consequences of financial reporting and disclosure regulation: A review and suggestions for future research.* Working paper, University of Chicago.

Liao, Q., T. Sellhorn and H.A. Skaife (2012), "The Cross-Country Comparability of IFRS Earnings and Book Values: Evidence from France and Germany", *Journal of International Accounting Research*, Spring, 11, 155–184.

Macías, M. and F. Muiño (2011), "Examining dual accounting systems in Europe", *The International Journal of Accounting*, 46, 51–78.

Navarro-Garcia, J.C. and F. Bastida (2010), "An empirical insight on Spanish listed companies' perceptions of International Financial Reporting Standards", *Journal of International Accounting, Auditing and Taxation*, 19, 110–120.

Nobes, C.W. (1998), "Towards a general model of the reasons for international differences in financial reporting", *Abacus*, 34(2), 162–187.

Nobes, C.W. (Ed.) (2001), "GAAP 2001: A survey of national accounting rules benchmarked against international accounting standards", *International Forum on Accountancy Development.*

Ohlson, J. and B. Juettner-Nauroth (2005), "Expected EPS and EPS growth as determinants of value", *Review of Accounting Studies,* 10, 349–365.

Pae, J., D. Thornton and M. Welker (2008), "Agency cost reduction associated with EU financial reporting reform", *Journal of International Accounting Research*, Spring, 51–75.

Sloan, R. (1996), "Do stock prices fully reflect information in accruals and cash flows about future earnings?", *The Accounting Review,* 71, 289–315.

Soderstrom, N.S. and K.J. Sun (2007), "IFRS adoption and accounting quality: a review", *European Accounting Review*, 16(4), 675–702.

Sucher, P. and I. Jindrichovska (2004), "Implementing IFRS: a case study of the Czech Republic", *Accounting in Europe*, 1(1), 109–141.

Tan, H., S. Wang and M. Welker (2011), "Analyst following and forecast accuracy after mandated IFRS adoptions", *Journal of Accounting Research,* 49, 1307–1357.

Tarca, A. (2004), "International convergence of accounting practices: Choosing between IAS and US GAAP", *Journal of International Financial Management and Accounting,* 15, 60–91.

Thorell, P. and G. Whittington (1994), "The harmonization of accounting within the EU Problems, perspectives and strategies", *European Accounting Review*, 3(2), 215–240.

Vellam, I. (2004), "Implementation of International Accounting Standards in Poland: can true convergence be achieved in practice?", *Accounting in Europe*, 1(1), 143–167.

Verrecchia, R. (2001), "Essays on disclosure", *Journal of Accounting and Economics,* 32, 91–180.

Verriest, A., A. Gaeremynck and D. Thornton (2010), *Corporate governance and properties of IFRS adoption.* INTACCT Working paper, Tilburg University.

Wang, C. (2011), *Accounting standards harmonization and financial statement comparability: Evidence from transnational information transfer.* Working paper, The Wharton School.

Watts, R. and J. Zimmermann (1986), *Positive Accounting Theory*, London, Prentice-Hall.

Weißenberger, B., A. Stahl and S. Vorstius (2004), "Changing from German GAAP to IFRS or US GAAP: a survey of German companies", *Accounting in Europe*, 1(1), 169–189.

Welker, M. (1995), "Disclosure policy, information asymmetry, and liquidity in equity markets", *Contemporary Accounting Research,* 11, 801–827.

Whittington, G. (2005), "The adoption of international standards in the European Union", *European Accounting Review*, 14(1), 127–153.

Wysocki, P. (2004), "Discussion of ultimate ownership, income management, and legal and extralegal institutions", *Journal of Accounting Research,* 42, 463–474.

Yip, R. Y. W. and D. Young (2012), "Does Mandatory IFRS Adoption Improve Information Comparability?", *The Accounting Review*, Forthcoming.

Yu, F. (2008), "Analyst coverage and earnings management", *Journal of Financial Economics*, 88, 245–271.

Zeghal, D., S. M. Chtourou and Y. M. Fourati (2012), "The effect of mandatory adoption of IFRS on earnings quality: evidence from the European Union", *Journal of International Accounting Research*, 11(2), 1–25.

Chapter 4

The Effect of Accounting Disclosure on the Firm's Cost of Capital

1. Introduction

The link between accounting information and the firm's cost of capital is one of the most fundamental issues in accounting and standard setters and regulators often refer to it.

Art. 1 of Regulation 1606/2002 states that its objective is "the adoption of international accounting standards with the view to [...] ensure a high degree of transparency and comparability of financial statements and hence an efficient functioning of the [...] capital market". As a result, one of the expected effects of the IAS/IFRS implementation in Europe is a reduction in the firm's cost of capital. A higher level of transparency in financial reporting should lower the estimation risk premium which arises in case of information asymmetries and, therefore, the firm's cost of capital.

As claimed by Neel Foster (2003), former member of the Financial Accounting Standards Board (FASB), "more information always equates to less uncertainty. In the context of financial information, the end result is that better disclosure results in a lower cost of capital".

The IAS/IFRS adoption in the European Union is also expected, through accounting standardization, to reduce possible errors in cross-country comparison of European companies due to different accounting systems. The adoption of the same accounting standard set within the European Union should improve comparability and, in this way, eliminate accounting measurement errors in pricing firms. As a result, the IAS/IFRS adoption at the European level is also expected to reduce cross-country differences in the cost of capital. If this is the case, the Regulator's intent of fostering an equal footing competition for financial resources among firms can be considered as reached.

Several studies have investigated the link between disclosure and the firm's cost of capital. Different from research which focuses on the usefulness of financial information to investors, these studies investigate the direct effects of accounting changes on firms.

2. Cost of capital and accounting information

While the claim that better disclosure results in lower cost of capital has intuitive appeal, there is little theoretical work on the hypothesized link.

In general, the economic theory underlying empirical studies on the relationship between accounting information and the cost of capital can be outlined as follows. Information asymmetries create costs by introducing adverse selection into transactions between buyers and sellers of firm shares. In real institutional settings, adverse selection typically manifests in reduced levels of liquidity for firm shares (Copeland and Galai 1983, Kyle 1985, Glosten and Milgrom 1985). To overcome the reluctance of potential investors to hold firm shares in illiquid markets, firms must issue capital at a discount. Discounting results in fewer proceeds to the firm and, hence, in a higher cost of capital.

A commitment to an increased level of disclosure reduces the possibility of information asymmetries arising either between the firm and its shareholders or among potential buyers and sellers of firm shares. This, in turn, should reduce the discount at which firm shares are sold, thus lowering the cost of issuing capital (Diamond and Verrecchia 1991, Baiman and Verrecchia 1996).

With regard to the notion of "increased levels of disclosure", the theory is sufficiently broad so as to allow either an increase in the quantity of disclosure or an increase in the quality of disclosure, or both. In addition, the theory makes no distinction as to how the information asymmetries arise (e.g. between a firm and its shareholders, among potential buyers and sellers of firm shares). The only requirement is that information asymmetries manifest themselves as a higher premium in the price at which trades are executed.

Different studies have provided theoretical links between accounting information and the cost of capital arising from information asymmetry.

Some of them suggest an indirect link between disclosure and firms' cost of capital based on market liquidity and adverse selection in the secondary market. Grossman and Stiglitz (1980), for instance, provide a model of information acquisition for risky investments, where an uninformed investor will buy information as long as the marginal benefit of doing so equals the marginal cost. Because investors demand a higher cost of capital to compensate for costly information acquisition, cost of capital will be lower if there is information about firm value available at little or no cost. Since accounting information is universally available at little or no cost, the Grossman and Stiglitz model suggests that the more informative accounting information is, the lower the cost of information acquisition will be. As a result, there will be more informed traders, less information asymmetry and lower cost of capital.

Easley and O'Hara (2004) develop an asset pricing model in which both public and private information affect asset returns. In their model, private information about a firm's future cash flows increases the risk to uninformed investors of holding a firm's stock because informed investors are better able to shift their portfolio weights to incorporate new information. Through their trades, the uninformed traders charge a risk premium to reflect their information disadvantage. Thus, the equilibrium price is lower if information asymmetry between the informed and uninformed traders is higher.

Some other studies explain the link between accounting information and cost of capital in terms of risk associated with mis-estimation of firms' return distribution parameters (Klein and Bawa 1976, Barry and Brown 1985, Coles and Loewenstein 1988, Clarkson and Thompson 1990, Handa and Linn 1993, Jorgensen and Kirschenheiter 2007). A common feature of these models is that the estimation risk associated with a firm's payoff distribution is priced by investors. Therefore, higher accounting information can lower a firm's cost of capital if it reduces such an estimation risk.

Lambert *et al.* (2007) have generalized and extended prior works on the estimation risk by examining whether and in what way accounting information about a firm manifests in its cost of capital. Their findings are particularly important as they suggest that a firm's beta factor is a function of its information quality and disclosures.

Lambert *et al.* develop a model which is consistent with the Capital Asset Pricing Model and demonstrate that the quality of accounting information can influence the cost of capital, both directly and indirectly.

The direct effect occurs because higher quality accounting information affects the market participants' assessments of the distribution of future cash flows. An indirect effect occurs because higher quality accounting information affects a firm's real decisions, which – in turn – influences its expected value and co-variances of firm cash flows.

In the direct effect category, Lambert *et al.* show that higher quality information reduces both the assessed variance of a firm's cash flows and their covariance with other firms' cash flows. This result builds on and extends prior works on "estimation risk" in finance (Brown 1979, Barry and Brown 1984 and 1985, Coles and Loewenstein 1988, and Coles *et al.* 1995). In this literature, information typically arises from a historical time series of return observations. Barry and Brown and Coles *et al.*, for instance, compare two information environments, one with the same amount of information (e.g., the same number of historical time series observations) available for all firms in the economy, and the other with more observations available just for one group of firms, showing that the betas of the "high information" securities are lower than they would be in the equal information case.

In the indirect effect category, Lambert *et al.* show that the quality of accounting information influences the cost of capital through its effect on a firm's real decisions. Many papers in agency theory have suggested that better financial reporting and/or corporate governance increases firm value by reducing the amount that managers appropriate for themselves (e.g., La Porta *et al.*, 1997; Lambert, 2001). Lambert *et al.* demonstrate that if better information reduces the amount of firm cash flows that managers appropriate for themselves, the improvements in disclosure not only increase firm price, but also reduce firm cost of capital. Furthermore, they demonstrate that information quality changes a firm's real decisions, which is likely to change the ratio of the expected future cash flows to the covariance of these cash flows with the sum of all the cash flows in the market, thus influencing the firm's cost of capital.

Finally, Lambert *et al.* show that increasing the quality of mandated disclosures should in general move the cost of capital closer to the risk-free rate for all firms in the economy. In addition to the effect of an individual firm's disclosures, there is also an externality from the disclosures of other firms, which may provide a rationale for disclosure regulation.

Some studies have specifically focused on the relation between cost of capital and conditional conservatism in accounting. Conditional conservatism imposes stronger verification requirements for the recognition of economic gains than economic losses, thus resulting in earnings that reflect losses faster than gains. This is referred to the asymmetric timeliness of earnings (Basu 1997).

Recent analytical work by Guay and Verrecchia (2007) and Suijs (2008) demonstrates that asymmetric reporting can affect a firm's market value and its cost of equity capital. More accurate bad news reporting reduces the discount that investors apply to firm value in the presence of uncertainty as well as the volatility of future stock prices which, in turn, lower the shareholders' investment risk.

Guay and Verrecchia (2007) articulate the mechanism underlying the predicted relation between conditional conservatism and cost of capital. In their model, uncertainty about the information structure leads to the appearance of risk premiums as investors place less weight on imprecise information signals, whereas fuller disclosure reduces the uncertainty about expected future cash flows and, therefore, lowers the cost of capital. Fuller disclosure is achieved via timely recognition of difficult-to-verify losses in the audited financial statements combined with voluntary strategic disclosure of good news through various other information channels, which are expected to flourish in the presence of conservative reporting (LaFond and Watts 2008).

Suijs (2008) suggests an alternative link between firm reporting policy and cost of capital. In his model, overlapping generations of shareholders invest in a firm with a life cycle that exceeds shareholders' investment horizons. In such a setting, more informative disclosure of bad news leads to a more efficient risk sharing across generations of investors which, in turn, lowers the cost of capital and increases the firm value.

3. Empirical literature on the link between accounting information and firms' cost of capital

As already discussed, there is extensive literature linking various characteristics of accounting information to proxies for the cost of capital. While the theory that relates the level of disclosure to the firm's cost of capital is compelling, so far the empirical results have been mixed.

Leuz and Verrecchia (2000) note that one potential explanation for the mixed results, aside from the difficulties of measuring the cost of capital directly and estimating this relation, is that most of the studies use data from firms publicly registered in the United States, where the disclosure environment under U.S. GAAP was already rich. Consequently, commitments to increased levels of disclosure were largely incremental, thereby leading to economic consequences that are difficult to substantiate empirically.

Botosan (1997) has investigated the relation between voluntary accounting information and the cost of capital. The cost of equity is derived from the accounting-based valuation formulae developed by Edwards and Bell (1961), Ohlson (1995) and Feltham and Ohlson (1995) and is then regressed on market beta, firm size and a self-constructed index of disclosure level. The index of disclosure level includes five categories of voluntary information identified by investors and financial analysts as useful in investment decision making: background information, summary of historical results, key non-financial statistics, projected information and management discussion and analysis. The regression involves US firms in the machinery industry and documents a significant relation between the disclosure level index and the firm's cost of capital, but only for firms with low analyst following.

Using a similar index for foreign firms trading in US equity markets, Botosan and Frost (1998) repeat Botosan's previous analysis and find a significant association between liquidity and timeliness, but not level of disclosure.

Botosan and Plumlee (2002) extend the results of Botosan (1997) to include larger, more heavily followed firms, across a diverse group of industries, over a number of years. They examine the association between the expected cost of equity capital and three types of disclosure: annual report, quarterly and other published reports and investor relations. They use four alternative estimates for the expected cost of equity capital and find that the cost of equity capital decreases in annual report disclosure level. The size of the difference in the cost of equity capital between the most and least forthcoming firms consists in approximately one-half to one percentage point, after controlling for market beta and firm size. Contrary to their expectations, findings document a positive association between the cost of equity capital and the level of more timely disclosures, such as the quarterly report. In this case, the size of the difference in cost of equity capital between the most and least forthcoming firms is approximately one to two percentage points, after controlling for market beta and firm size. This result, though contrary to that predicted by theory, is however consistent with managers' claims that more timely disclosures increase the cost of equity capital, possibly through increased stock price volatility. Finally, no association is found between the cost of equity capital and the level of investor relation activities.

Botosan and Plumlee (2005) examine the relation between the cost of equity capital and the information attributes posited by Easley and O'Hara (2004). In the Easley and O'Hara's model, the cost of equity capital is affected by the following attributes of information: the proportion of the information set that is private versus public *(composition)*; the fraction of investors who are informed *(dissemination)*; the overall precision of the information set *(precision)*; the existence of information *(existence)*. Easley and O'Hara demonstrate that the cost of equity capital is increasing in the composition of the information set and decreasing in its dissemination and precision. Botosan and Plumlee document results consistent with the predictions of Easley and O'Hara as all the proxies for cost of equity capital increase in composition and decrease in dissemination and precision.

Some studies have focused on the relation between the cost of equity and a variety of proxies for earnings quality. Bhattacharya *et al.* (2003), for instance, find a link between three earnings quality measures (earnings aggressiveness, loss avoidance and earnings smoothing) and a proxy for the expected cost of equity in country-level tests. Francis *et al.* (2004) relate seven measures of earnings quality to a proxy for the expected cost of equity implied by Value Line analyst estimates of target share price and dividend growth. Four of the measures are accounting-based (accrual quality, earnings persistence, predictability and smoothness) and three market-based (relevance, timeliness and conservatism). Evidence reports that higher earnings quality is associated with lower implied expected costs of capital, with the greatest effects being associated with lower accounting-based proxies.

In contrast, Cohen (2003) does not find any association between earnings quality and the cost of equity in tests that take into account the endogeneity of accounting choice.

Finally, Barth *et al.* (2011) provide evidence that firms with more transparent earnings enjoy a lower cost of capital. By using an earnings transparency measure that permits cross-sectional and inter-temporal variation to the extent in which earnings and change in earnings co-vary contemporaneously with stock returns, they show that firms with more transparent earnings have lower cost of capital as reflected in subsequent returns and portfolio mean returns, after controlling for the Fama-French and momentum factors. They also report that more transparent earnings are significantly negatively associated with the expected cost of capital.

To the extent that IAS/IFRS is deemed to represent a set of high-quality accounting standards, their results provide evidence consistent with high quality financial reporting lowering the cost of equity capital.

A stream of empirical research has focused on conditional conservatism showing that conditional conservatism is associated with positive economic outcomes (Bushman, Piotroski, and Smith 2007, Ahmed and Duellman 2008, LaFond and Watts 2008, Francis and Martin 2010, Lara *et al.* 2011). As mentioned above, conditional conservatism imposes stronger verification requirements for the recognition of economic gains than economic losses, thus resulting in earnings that reflect losses faster than gains. This is referred to the asymmetric timeliness of earnings (Basu 1997).

Lara *et al.* (2011), for instance, test the association between conditional conservatism and the firm cost of equity capital for a large sample of US firms during the period 1975 to 2003. They use a firm-specific measure of conservatism based on the work of Callen, Segal and Hope (2010) and document a robust negative association between conditional conservatism and cost of capital, consistently with Guay and Verrecchia (2007) and Suijs (2008).

Several studies have focused on the relation between disclosure and different market variables posited to be associated with the cost of capital such as bid-ask spreads, trading volume in firm shares, and share price volatility. As previously discussed, the relation between these proxies and the firm's cost of capital is well established in theory and several studies have also provided evidence that information asymmetry and illiquidity are reflected in stock returns.

The bid-ask spread is commonly thought to measure information asymmetry explicitly. The reason for this is that the bid-ask spread addresses the adverse selection problem that arises from firm shares transaction occurring in the presence of asymmetrically informed investors. Less information asymmetry implies less adverse selection, which, in turn, implies a smaller bid-ask spread.

An alternative, and perhaps less explicit proxy for adverse selection is trading volume in firm shares. Trading volume has been used as a measure of liquidity in that it captures the willingness of some investors who hold firm shares to sell and the willingness of others to buy (Easley 1996 and Grammig, Scjiereck and Theissen 2001). This willingness to transact in firm shares should be inversely related to the existence of information asymmetries. Trading volume, however, can be influenced by a host of other factors unrelated to information, such as portfolio rebalancing, liquidity shock and changes in risk preference. Consequently, trading volume may not exclusively capture information asymmetry among investors.

Finally, the use of share price volatility as a proxy for information asymmetry involves that smooth transitions in share prices, hence low levels of volatility, suggest the absence of information asymmetries between the firm and shareholders or among investors (Lang and Lundholm 1993). As with trading volume, however, volatility is influenced by many factors unrelated to information asymmetry.

Healy, Hutton and Palepu (1999), for instance, show that firms with sustained increases in disclosure ratings exhibit improvement in a number of variables, including the bid-ask spread. Greenstein and Sami (1994), Boone (1998) and Piotroski (1999), use bid-ask spread to assess the impact of specific mandated reporting changes on the cost of equity. Greenstein and Sami (1994) focus on the impact of the SEC's segment disclosure requirements and provide limited evidence that segment disclosure regulation had an impact on the market microstructure as represented by bid-ask spreads. Piotroski (1999) also focuses on segment reporting and finds that expanded segment disclosures are associated with analysts' positive forecast revisions and with an increase in the earnings' capitalization rate, while there are no significant changes in liquidity.

Boone (1998) compares bid-ask spreads on common stocks traded on the NASDAQ market before and after a fair value measure of oil and gas reserves was released by oil and gas firms and finds that the size of the spread declined significantly in the year following the disclosure of reserve values. Furthermore, the amount of such a decline was statistically associated with the absolute value of the difference between the book value of oil reserves and the discounted present value of oil reserves, which is used as a proxy for the degree of information asymmetry.

Bartov and Bodnar (1996) focus on trade volume and examine whether differences in information asymmetry explain more informative accounting choices. They focus on SFAS No. 52 (Foreign Currency Translation) and show that managers wishing to maximize the value of their firms have incentive to reduce the degree of information asymmetry by switching to newly available accounting techniques which make financial statements more informative to investors. Tests on the choice of functional currency among US multinational firms support these predictions after controlling for variables such as the debt-to-equity ratio, interest coverage, size, and the relative size of the foreign currency adjustment in the financial statements.

Bushee and Noe (2000) demonstrate that the effect of disclosure on volatility is complex and may depend on the type of investors attracted to the firm. Firms with a higher disclosure ranking have greater institutional ownership and yearly improvements in the disclosure ranking are associated with increases in ownership primarily by "transient" institutions, which are characterized by aggressive trading based on short-term strategies. In addition, firms with disclosure ranking improvements resulting in higher transient ownership are found to experience subsequent increases in stock return volatility.

Finally, some studies have explored the link between the quality of accounting information and proxies for the cost of debt. Because of data availability, these studies are limited to firms with available debt cost or bond rating data. Welker (1995) and Sengupta (1998), for instance, use analyst ratings of the firm's overall disclosure policy and report that firms with higher disclosure ratings have, on average, lower bid-ask spreads and a lower cost of debt at the time of issue, respectively. For a sample of 120 firms, Beatty *et al.* (2002) find that the debt cost of capital is lower if the loan agreement contains debt covenants that exclude voluntary accounting changes. Based on a broader sample of firms, Francis *et al.* (2005) also find that firms with higher earnings quality have higher bond ratings and lower *ex post* debt interest costs.

4. Research on the effects of IAS/IFRS adoption on the cost of capital

Empirical research relating the cost of capital to commitment to higher financial reporting quality has typically focused on a firm's commitment to apply a set of accounting standards or on a firm's decision to cross-list its shares on a foreign stock exchange (Leuz and Verrecchia, 2000; Leuz, 2003; Daske *et al.*, 2008).

In the first research stream, some studies have focused on a comparison between IAS/IFRS or US GAAP, on the one hand, and domestic GAAP on the other hand. Auer (1996), for instance, investigates changes in share price volatility for Swiss firms that switched from Swiss GAAP to European Directives or IAS. Results show a significant change in the variance of abnormal returns for firms which switched to the European Directives or IAS but no statistically significant differences in the variance of abnormal returns for earnings based on European Directives or IAS, thus suggesting that IAS-based earnings do not convey higher information than European Directives to investors.

Leuz and Verrecchia (2000) focus on German firms that switched from German GAAP to IAS or US GAAP. They find that bid-ask spreads are lower and trading volumes higher for firms employing international standards, but fail to detect less share volatility around the switch.

Motivated by the debate about globally uniform accounting standards, Leuz (2003) also investigates whether firms using US GAAP vis-à-vis IAS exhibit differences in several proxies for information asymmetry. He focuses on German firms producing financial statements in accordance with either IAS or US GAAP by virtue of their listing on the "New Market", a German market segment for growth firms in emerging industries. Findings show that the choice between IAS and US GAAP has no measurable consequences on the proxies used for the information asymmetry component of the cost of equity – namely, the bid-ask spreads and trading volume – of these firms. At least for New Market firms, the choice between IAS and US GAAP appears to be of little consequence for information asymmetry and market liquidity. Subsequent analyses of analysts' forecast dispersion, initial public offering under-pricing, and firms' standard choices corroborate these findings. These findings do not therefore provide support to the widespread claims that US GAAP produce financial statements of higher informational quality than IAS/IFRS.

Building on Leuz and Verrecchia (2000), Daske (2006) uses a set of German firms that adopted IAS/IFRS or US GAAP standards and investigates the potential economic benefits of this reporting strategy by analysing their cost of equity capital through the use and customisation of available implied estimation methods. Evidence from the 1993–2002 period fails, however, to document a lower expected cost of equity capital for firms applying international standards. In fact, during the transition period the expected cost of equity capital appears, rather, to have increased under non-local accounting standards.

Cuijpers and Buijink (2005) examine the determinants and consequences of voluntary adoption of IAS/IFRS and US GAAP by firms listed and domiciled in the European Union on three proxies for information asymmetry: analyst following, cost of equity capital, and uncertainty among analysts and investors as measured by forecast dispersion and shock return volatility. They document a positive effect of non-local GAAP adoption on analyst following, but fail to provide evidence of a lower cost of capital for non-local GAAP adopters. Contrary to expectations, uncertainty among analysts and investors appears to be higher for firms using IAS/IFRS or US GAAP than for firms using local GAAP. However, by comparing early and late adopters, they find some evidence that suggests that benefits take some time to fully materialize.

Kim and Shi (2010) also investigate the implied cost of equity capital effect of voluntary IAS/IFRS adoption, and whether and how this effect is associated with the efficacy of a country's institutional infrastructure around the world from 1998 to 2004. Findings show that voluntary IAS/IFRS adoption firms significantly lower the cost of equity capital irrespective of a country's institutional infrastructure, even though the capital-reducing effect is greater in countries with stronger institutional infrastructures.

Empirical research has generally focused on the average effects around IAS/IFRS adoption. Daske *et al.* (2012) focus, instead, on firm-level heterogeneity in the effects around the IAS/IFRS adoption recognizing that firms have considerable discretion in how they implement IAS/IFRS. Some firms may make very few changes and adopt IAS/IFRS more in name, while for others the change in standards could be part of a strategy to increase their commitment to transparency. They classify firms into 'label' and 'serious' adopters by using firm-level changes in reporting incentives, actual reporting behaviour, and the external reporting environment around the switch to IAS/IFRS and then analyze whether capital-market effects are different across 'serious' and 'label' adoptions. While capital-market effects around voluntary IAS/IFRS adoptions are on average often insignificant, they find considerable heterogeneity in the effects. 'Serious' adoptions are in fact associated with an increase in liquidity and a decline in cost of capital, which is not the case for 'label' adoptions. Similar results are obtained around the mandatory IAS/IFRS adoption. These findings therefore suggest caution when interpreting capital-market effects around the IAS/IFRS adoption, as they may reflect changes in reporting incentives or broader changes in firms' reporting strategies, and not just in the standards.

Kim, Tsui and Yi (2011) also investigate the effect of voluntary adoption of IAS/IFRS, but focus on loan contracting around the world providing evidence that banks consider the quality of financial reporting when assessing credit risk. Using a sample of non-US borrowers from 40 countries during 1997 through 2005, they investigate the effect of the voluntary adoption of IAS/IFRS on price and non-price terms of loan contracts as well as on loan ownership structure in the international loan market. Their results reveal that banks charge lower loan rates to IAS/IFRS adopters than to non-adopters. The difference in loan rates in excess of a benchmark rate between the two groups is about 20 basis points for all loans and nearly 31 basis points for London Interbank Offered Rate (LIBOR)-based loans. Moreover, banks impose more favourable non-price terms on IAS/IFRS adopters, that is, less restrictive covenants. They also provide evidence suggesting that banks are more willing to extend credit to IAS/IFRS adopters through larger loans and longer maturities. Finally, IAS/IFRS adopters are found to attract significantly more foreign lenders participating in loan syndicates than non-adopters.

5. Research on the effects of the mandatory IAS/IFRS adoption on the cost of capital

As perhaps one of the most significant financial reporting reforms in recent years, the mandatory IAS/IFRS adoption in the EU has given rise to substantial controversy.

On one hand, skeptics of the mandatory IAS/IFRS adoption argue that given the importance of institutional arrangements on the effectiveness of new accounting rules (e.g., Ball *et al.* 2000; Burgstahler *et al.* 2006), and the substantial variation in institutional arrangements across the European Union countries, the potential benefits of the mandatory IAS/IFRS adoption are likely to vary depending on whether the new rules are effectively enforced. Consistent with this argument, standard setters recognized that a sound financial reporting infrastructure must be built on "an enforcement or oversight mechanism that ensures that the principles as laid out by the accounting and auditing standards are followed" (Tweedie and Seidenstein 2005). In addition, some observers have questioned whether a uniform set of standards adequately accommodates the economic and political differences across countries (e.g. Sunder 2007).

On the other hand, prior research has suggested that, given proper implementation and enforcement, the mandatory IAS/IFRS adoption are likely to reduce the cost of equity capital through at least two mechanisms.

The first mechanism is increased financial disclosure. IAS/IFRS typically requires greater disclosure than local accounting standards. The information asymmetry literature suggests that greater disclosure mitigates the adverse selection problem and enhances liquidity, thereby reducing the cost of equity through lower transaction costs and/or stronger demand for a firm's securities (Amihud and Mendelson 1986, Diamond and Verrecchia 1991, Easley and O'Hara 2004). The estimation risk literature also predicts that firms with greater information disclosure have lower forward-looking betas, which leads to a lower cost of equity (Barry and Brown 1985, Lambert *et al.* 2007). These theoretical predictions find support in several empirical studies, including Botosan (1997) and Francis *et al.* (2005).

As mentioned above, adverse selection refers to a market process in which investors recognize that the market is not a "level playing field" and they either withdraw from the market or lower the amount they are willing to pay for any security, thus increasing the firms' cost of capital.

The second mechanism through which the mandatory IAS/IFRS adoption could reduce the cost of equity is enhanced information comparability. A uniform set of accounting standards can result in enhanced comparability of financial information across firms, especially for firms located in different countries. Enhanced information comparability can reduce the costs associated with investors using information and, in turn, reduce information asymmetry and/or estimation risk, leading to a lower cost of equity. Barth *et al.* (1999) develop a similar argument by showing that international accounting harmonization is likely to reduce the expertise acquisition costs incurred when foreign investors interpret financial statements prepared under domestic accounting standards. Furthermore, the enhanced comparability effects of IAS/IFRS convergence may also bring about positive information externalities. As the value of one firm is correlated with that of another firm, the information disclosed by firms in one country becomes more comparable and, hence, more useful in valuing firms in another country if both countries adopt IAS/IFRS, thus reducing estimation risk and the cost of equity capital.

Such externalities are magnified as the number of countries converging to IAS/IFRS increases. These effects of improved comparability are consistent with Covrig *et al.* (2007), who found that average foreign mutual fund ownership is higher among voluntary IAS/IFRS adopters as they provide more information or information in a more familiar form to foreign investors. Similarly, Amiram (2009) documents that foreign equity investment increases after the IAS/IFRS adoption, particularly for countries with low corruption and strong investor protection. This result is consistent with Khurana and Michas (2011) and Shima and Gordon (2011). Chen *et al.* (2009) and Màrquez-Ramos (2011) show that foreign direct investment also increases following the IAS/IFRS mandatory adoption and that the size of this effect depends on country institutions.

Prior research on the relation between disclosure and the cost of capital has largely been based on voluntary adoption of IAS/IFRS. The distinction between commitment and voluntary disclosure is quite relevant for studies on the cost of equity since the former is independent of the content of the information, whereas the latter is a decision taken by the firm.

While providing useful insights, the findings on voluntary IAS/IFRS adoption cannot therefore be generalized in the case of the mandatory IAS/IFRS adoption. This is because voluntary adopters self-select to follow IAS/IFRS after considering the related costs and benefits, with the cost of capital effects being only one of them, whereas mandatory adopters in the European Union switched to IAS/IFRS because this was required by Regulation 1606/2002. As a result, whether or not the mandatory IAS/IFRS adoption reduces the cost of capital for mandatory adopters has become an empirical question.

One of the first studies on the effects of the mandatory IAS/IFRS adoption in Europe is provided by Palea (2007), who focuses on the bank industry showing that in the period immediately subsequent to the IAS/IFRS mandatory adoption banks experienced a reduction in their cost of equity.

Li (2010) explores the cost of equity effects of the mandatory IAS/IFRS adoption in the EU by deriving the cost of equity from the models by Claus and Thomas (2001), Gerbhardt *et al.* (2001), Gode and Mohanram (2003) and Easton (2004), finding that in 2005, on average, mandatory adopters experienced a significant reduction in the cost of equity of 47 basis points. Additional analysis suggests, however, that mandating IAS/IFRS has a significant cost of equity impact only in countries with strong enforcement mechanisms, consistent with the quality of legal enforcement being an important factor for effective accounting changes. While mandatory adoption significantly lowers the firms' cost of equity on average, the effects depend however on the strength of the countries' legal enforcement. Furthermore, Li provides further insight into whether the effects on cost of equity are due to increased disclosure and/or enhanced comparability. She uses the number of additional disclosures required by IAS/IFRS relative to local standards as a measure of increased disclosure and the number of inconsistencies between IAS/IFRS and local standards as a measure of enhanced comparability and finds evidence consistent with both increased disclosure and enhanced comparability influencing the cost of equity effects of the mandatory IAS/IFRS adoption.

Similarly, Daske *et al.* (2008) examine the effect of the mandatory IAS/IFRS adoption on market liquidity, cost of capital and Tobin's. They analyse the effects of adopting IAS/IFRS in 26 countries, both in Europe and worldwide, and document an increase in market liquidity around the time of the IAS/IFRS adoption. They also find a decrease in firms' cost of equity and an increase in equity valuation, but only if prior effects to the adoption date are accounted for. Taken as a whole, their evidence suggests modest, but economically significant capital market benefits around the IAS/IFRS mandatory adoption. However, such market benefits occur only in countries where firms have incentives to be transparent and where legal enforcement is strong, suggesting once more that enforcement regimes and firms' reporting incentives play a major role in achieving capital market benefits from the IAS/IFRS adoption. Capital market effects of IAS/IFRS adoption are also found to be larger for firms in countries with lower quality domestic standards and that differ more from IAS/IFRS. This result is in line with Armstrong *et al.* (2010) who find that the positive reaction to IAS/IFRS adoption is larger for firms with lower levels of information quality prior to IAS/IFRS implementation and higher pre-adoption information asymmetry.

Landsman *et al.* (2012) focus on countries adopting IAS/IFRS not only in Europe, but worldwide and examine whether the information content of earnings announcements, measured by abnormal return volatility and abnormal trading volume, increase following the mandatory IAS/IFRS adoption, as well as the conditions and mechanisms through which increases occur. Findings suggest that information content of earnings announcements increased in 16 countries that mandated IAS/IFRS relative to 11 that maintained domestic accounting standards, although the effect of the mandatory adoption depended on the strength of legal enforcement in the adopting country. Their findings also provide evidence that the IAS/IFRS adoption increased information content through reducing reporting lag, increasing analyst following and increasing foreign investment.

Finally, Florou and Kosi (2011) investigate the effects of the mandatory IAS/IFRS adoption on the cost of corporate debt. Using a global sample of public and private debt issues completed during 2000–2007, they find that mandatory IAS/IFRS adopters are more likely to issue public bonds than to borrow privately. Moreover, IAS/IFRS adopters pay lower bond yield spreads, whereas no significant effect on the cost of private loans is found. They document that the mandatory IAS/IFRS adopters are more likely to raise debt from a larger pool of capital at a lower cost. Furthermore, the mandatory IAS/IFRS adoption is beneficial primarily for bond investors, who rely more on financial statements and have much less monitoring and renegotiating privileges compared to private lenders. The positive consequences of IAS/IFRS for debt financing are however present only in countries with stricter rule enforcement, higher control of corruption and lower financial risk, thus providing once more evidence that mandatory financial reporting under IAS/IFRS has beneficial effects only when the country institutions are strong.

Viewed together, evidence on the effects of IAS/IFRS financial reporting on the cost of capital suggests overall beneficial effects from their mandatory adoption.

Empirical research supports, in general, the notion that adopting IAS/IFRS increases market liquidity, decreases transaction costs for investors, lowers cost of capital, and facilitates international capital formation and flows. However, research has also shown that these effects differ according to the level of legal regulatory enforcement and firms' incentives. Adoption of IFRS is not the only factor which affects the cost of capital. Many studies have cited a range of other factors that might also outweigh any beneficial effects of the IAS/IFRS adoption. Ball (2006), as well as Soderstrom and

Sun (2007), note that such variables include: extent and nature of government involvement in the economy; government involvement in financial reporting practices such as political influence of managers, corporations, labour unions, and banks; legal systems such as common law versus code law and shareholder litigation rules; securities regulation and regulatory bodies; depth of financial markets; financial market structure, such as closeness of the relationship between banks and clients; the roles of the press, financial analysts, and ratings agencies; size of the corporate sector; structure of corporate governance such as relative roles of labour, management, and capital; extent of private versus public ownership of corporations, of family-controlled businesses and of corporate membership in related company groups; extent of financial intermediation; role of small shareholders versus institutions and corporate insiders; use of financial statement information, including earnings, in management compensation; status, independence, training, and compensation of auditors.

Empirical research has confirmed that such variables play a key role in determining capital market effects of adopting IAS/IFRS and have actually led to an application of IAS/IFRS which is not uniform across Europe, with consequences on accounting quality both in absolute and relative terms. Since accounting quality is a function of the firm's overall institutional setting, including the legal and political system of the country in which the firms reside, there is in fact enough evidence suggesting that cross-country differences in accounting are likely to remain also after the IAS/IFRS adoption.

References

Aboody, D., J. Hughes and J. Liu, "Earnings quality, insider trading, and cost of capital", *Journal of Accounting Research*, 43(5).

Ahmed, A. S. and S. Duellman (2007), "Evidence on the role of accounting conservatism in corporate governance", *Journal of Accounting and Economics*, 43, 411–437.

Ahmed, A. S. and S. Duellman (2008), *Evidence on the role of accounting conservatism in monitoring managers' investment decisions*. Working paper, Texas A & M University.

Amihud, Y. and H. Mendelson (1986), "Asset pricing and the bid-ask spread", *Journal of Financial Economics*, 17, 223–249.

Amihud, Y. and H. Mendelson (1988), "Liquidity and asset prices: financial management implications", *Financial Management*, 17, 5–15.

Amihud, Y. (2002), "Illiquidity and stock returns", *Journal of Financial Markets*, 5, 31–56.

Amihud, Y. and H. Mendelson (2008), "Liquidity, the value of the firm, and corporate finance", *Journal of Applied Corporate Finance*, 20, 32–45.

Amiram, D. (2009), *Financial information globalization and foreign investment decisions.* Working paper, University of North Carolina.

Ang, A. and J. Liu (2004), "How to discount cash flows with time-varying expected returns", *Journal of Finance*, 59, 2,745–2,783.

Armstrong, C., M. Barth, A. Jagolinzer and E. Riedl (2010), "Market reaction to the adoption of IFRS in Europe", *The Accounting Review*, 85(1), 31–61.

Auer, K.V. (1996), "Capital market reactions to earnings announcements: empirical evidence on the difference in the information content of IAS-based earnings and EC-directives-based earnings", *The European Accounting Review*, 5(4), 587–623.

Bailey, W., G.A. Karolyi and C. Salva (2006), "The economic consequences of increased disclosure: evidence from international cross-listings", *Journal of Financial Economics*, 81, 175–213.

Baiman, S. and R. Verrecchia (1996), "The relation among capital markets, financial disclosure, production efficiency, and insider trading", *Journal of Accounting Research*, Spring, 1–22.

Ball, R., S.P. Kothari and A. Robin (2000), "The effect of international institutional factors on properties of accounting earnings", *Journal of Accounting and Economics*, 29, 1–51.

Ball, R., S.P. Kothari, and A. Robin (2004), "The effect of international institutional factors on properties of accounting earnings", in C.W. Nobes, *Developments in international accounting-general issues and classification*, Cheltenham, UK and Northampton, Mass.: Elgar, 195–245.

Ball, R. (2006), "IFRS: pros and cons for investors", *Accounting and Business Research*, International Accounting Policy Forum, 5–27.

Barry, C.B. and S.J. Brown (1984), "Differential information and the small firm effect", *Journal of Financial Economics*, 13, 283–294.

Barry, C.B. and S.J. Brown (1985), "Differential information and security market equilibrium", *Journal of Financial and Quantitative Analysis*, 20, 407–422.

Barth, M.E., W.H. Beaver and W.R. Landsman (1998), "Relative valuation roles of equity book value and net income as a function of financial health", *Journal of Accounting and Economics*, 25, 1–34.

Barth, M.E., W.H. Beaver, J.M. Hand and W.R. Landsman (1999), "Accruals, cash flows and equity values", *Review of Accounting Studies*, 4, 205–229.

Barth, M.E., W.H. Beaver, J.M. Hand and W.R. Landsman (2005), "Accruals, accounting based valuation models, and the prediction of equity values", *Journal of Accounting, Auditing, and Finance*, 20, 311–345.

Barth, M.E., L.D. Hodder and S.R. Stubben (2008), "Fair value accounting for liabilities and own credit risk", *The Accounting Review*, 83, 629–664.

Barth, M.E. and K. Schipper (2008), "Financial reporting transparency", *Journal of Accounting, Auditing, and Finance*, 23, 173–190.

Barth, M.E., Y. Konchithcki and W.R. Landsman (2011), "Cost of capital and earnings transparency". Working paper, *Research Paper Series*, May.

Bartov, E. and G. Bodnar (1996), "Alternative accounting methods, information asymmetry and liquidity: theory and evidence", *The Accounting Review,* July, 397–418.

Basu, S. (1997), "The conservatism principle and the asymmetric timeliness of earnings", *Journal of Accounting and Economics*, December, 3–37.

Basu, S. (2004), "What do we learn from two new accounting-based stock market anomalies?", *Journal of Accounting and Economics*, December, 333–348.

Basu, S. and S. Markov (2004), "Loss function assumptions in rational expectations tests on financial analysts' earnings forecasts", *Journal of Accounting and Economics*, December, 171–203.

Beatty, A., K. Ramesh and J. Weber (2002), "The importance of accounting changes in debt contracts: the cost of flexibility in covenant calculations", *Journal of Accounting and Economics*, 29, 2.005–2.027.

Bhattacharya, U., H. Daouk and M. Welker (2003), "The world price of earnings opacity", *The Accounting Review*, 78, 641–678.

Boone, J. (1998), "Oil and Gas Reserve Value Disclosures and Bid-Ask Spreads." *Journal of Accounting and Public Policy,* Spring, 55–84.

Botosan, C.A. (1997), "Disclosure level and the cost of equity capital", *The Accounting Review*, 72, 323–349.

Botosan, C.A. and C. Frost (1998), *Regulation, disclosure and market liquidity*. Working paper, Washington University.

Botosan, C.A. and M. Plumlee (2002), "A re-examination of disclosure level and expected cost of equity capital", *Journal of Accounting Research*, 40, 21–40.

Botosan, C. and M. Plumlee (2005), "Are information attributes priced?", *The Accounting Review,* 80(1), 21–53.

Botosan, C., M. Plumlee and Y. Xie (2004), "The role of private information precision in determining cost of equity capital", *Review of Accounting Studies,* 9, 233–259.

Brown, S. (1979), "The effect of estimation risk on capital market equilibrium", *Journal of Financial and Quantitative Analysis*, 15, 215–220.

Brüggemann, U., J.-M. Hitz and T. Sellhorn (2012), "Intended and unintended consequences of mandatory IFRS adoption: a review of extant evidence and suggestions for future research", *European Accounting Review*, 1–37.

Burgstahler, D., L. Hail and C. Leuz (2006), "The importance of reporting incentives: earnings management in European private and public firms", *The Accounting Review*, 81(5), 983–1016.

Burgstahler, D. and M. Earnes (2006), "Management of earnings and analysts' forecasts to achieve zero and small positive earnings surprise", *Journal of Business Finance and Accounting*, 33(5–6), 633–652.

Bushee, B. and C. Noe (2000), "Corporate disclosure practices, institutional investors, and stock return volatility", *Journal of Accounting research*, 38, 171–202.

Bushman, R., Q. Chen, E. Engel and A. Smith (2004), "Financial accounting information, organizational complexity and corporate governance systems", *Journal of Accounting and Economics*, 37, 167–201.

Bushman, R.M., J.D. Piotroski and A.J. Smith (2007), *Capital allocation and timely accounting recognition of economic losses: international evidence.* Working paper, University of Chicago.

Callen, J.L. and D. Segal (2009), "A variance decomposition primer for accounting researchers", *Journal of Accounting, Auditing and Finance*, forthcoming.

Callen, J.L., D. Segal and O.-K. Hope (2010), "The pricing of conservative accounting and the measurement of conservatism at the firm-year level", *Review of Accounting Studies*, 15, 145–178.

Campbell, J. (1996), "Understanding risk and return", *Journal of Political Economy*, 104, 298–345.

Campbell, J.Y., M. Lettau, B.G. Malkiel and Y. Xu (2001), "Have individual stocks become more volatile? An empirical exploration of idiosyncratic risk", *Journal of Finance*, 56, 1–43.

Carhart, M.M. (1997), "On persistence in mutual fund performance", *Journal of Finance*, 52, 57–82.

Chen, K.C.W. and F. Tang (2009), *Do firms use the unrealized gains mandated by IFRS to increase executive cash compensation? Evidence from family-owned property companies in Hong Kong.* Working paper, Hong Kong University of Science and Technology.

Chordia, T., R. Roll and A. Subrahmanyam (2000), "Co-movements in bid-ask spreads and market depth", *Financial Analysts Journal*, 56, 23–27.

Clarkson, P. and R. Thompson (1990), "The empirical estimates of beta when investors face estimation risk", *Journal of Finance*, 45, 431–453.

Claus, J. and J. Thomas (2001), "Equity premia as low as three percent? Evidence from analysts' earnings forecasts for domestic and international stock markets", *Journal of Finance*, 56(5), 1629–1666.

Cochran, J.H. (2005), *Asset Pricing*, Princeton University Press, Princeton, New Jersey.

Cohen, D. (2003), *Quality of financial reporting choice: determinants and economic consequences.* Working paper, Northwestern University.

Coles, J. and U. Loewenstein (1988), "Equilibrium pricing and portfolio composition in the presence of uncertain parameters", *Journal of Financial Economics*, 279–303.

Coles, J., U. Loewenstein and J. Suay (1995), "On equilibrium pricing under parameter uncertainty", *The Journal of Financial and Quantitative Analysis*, 30, 347–374.
Collins, D. W. and S. P. Kothari (1989), "An analysis of intertemporal and cross-sectional determinants of earnings response coefficients", *Journal of Accounting and Economics*, 11, 143–181.
Collins, D. W., E. L. Maydew and I. S. Weiss (1997), "Changes in the value-relevance of earnings & equity book values over the past forty years", *Journal of Accounting and Economics*, 24, 39–67.
Copeland, T. and D. Galai (1983), "Information effects on the bid-ask spread", *Journal of Finance*, 1457–1469.
Core, J. E., W. R. Guay and R. S. Verdi (2008), "Is accruals quality a priced risk factor?", *Journal of Accounting and Economics*, 46, 2–22.
Covrig, V., M. DeFond and M. Hung (2007), "Home bias, foreign mutual fund holdings, and the voluntary adoption of International Accounting Standards", *Journal of Accounting Research*, 45(1), 41–70.
Cuijpers, R. and W. Buijink (2005), "Voluntary adoption of non-local GAAP in the European Union: A study of determinants and consequences", *European Accounting Review*, 14, 487–524.
Daske, H. (2006), "Economic benefits of adopting IFRS or US-GAAP: Have the expected costs of equity capital really decreased?", *Journal of Business Finance and Accounting*, 33(3–4), 329–373.
Daske, H., L. Hail, C. Leuz and R. Verdi (2008), "Mandatory IFRS reporting around the world: early evidence on the economic consequences", *Journal of Accounting Research*, 46(5), 1085–1142.
Daske, H., L. Hail, C. Leuz and R. Verdi (2012), *Adopting a label: heterogeneity in the economic consequences around IAS/IFRS adoptions.* Working paper.
Dechow, P. and I. Dichev (2002), "The quality of accruals and earnings: the role of accrual estimation errors", *The Accounting Review*, 77, supplement, 35–59.
Dhaliwal, D., S. Heitzman and O. Z. Li (2007), "Taxes, leverage, and the cost of equity capital", *Journal of Accounting Research*, 44, 691–723.
Diamond, D. W. and R. E. Verrecchia (1991), "Disclosure, liquidity, and the cost of capital", *Journal of Finance*, 46, 1.325–1.359.
Dye, R. (1990), "Mandatory versus voluntary disclosure: the cases of real and financial externalities", *The Accounting Review*, 65(1), 1–24.
Easley, D., S. Hvidkjaer and M. O'Hara (2002), "Is Information risk a determinant of asset returns?", *Journal of Finance*, 57, 2.185–2.221.
Easley, D., N. Kiefer, M. O'Hara and J. Paperman (1996), "Liquidity, information, and infrequently traded stocks", *Journal of Finance*, September, 1405–1436.
Easley, D. and M. O'Hara (2004), "Information and the cost of capital", *Journal of Finance*, 59, 1.553–1.583.
Easton, P. D. (2004), "PE ratios, PEG ratios, and estimating the implied expected rate of return on equity capital", *The Accounting Review*, 79, 73–95.

Easton, P. and T. Harris (1991), "Earnings as an explanatory variable for return", *Journal of Accounting Research*, 29, 19–36.

Easton, P. and S. Monahan (2005), "An evaluation of accounting-based measures of expected returns", *The Accounting Review*, 80, 501–538.

Easton, P. and J. Pae (2004), "Accounting conservatism and the relation between returns and accounting data", *Review of Accounting Studies*, 9, 495–521.

Ecker, F., J. Francis, I. Kim, P.M. Olsson and K. Schipper (2006), "A returns-based representation of earnings quality", *The Accounting Review*, 81, 749–780.

Edwards, E. and P. Bell (1961), *The theory and measurement of business income*, Berkeley, CA, University of California Press.

Elton, E. (1999), "Expected return, realized return, and asset pricing tests", *Journal of Finance*, 54, 1999–1220.

Fama, E.F. and K.R. French (1992), "The cross-section of expected stock returns", *Journal of Finance*, 47, 427–465.

Fama, E.F. and K.R. French (1993), "Common risk factors in the returns of stocks and bonds", *Journal of Financial Economics*, 33, 3–56.

Fama, E.F. and K.R. French (1997), "Industry costs of equity", *Journal of Financial Economics*, 43, 153–193.

Fama, E.F. and K.R. French (1998), "Taxes, financing decisions, and firm value", *Journal of Finance*, 53, 819–843.

Fama, E.F. and K.R. French (2002), "The equity premium", *Journal of Finance*, 57, 637–659.

Fama, E.F. and J.D. MacBeth (1973), "Risk, return, and equilibrium: empirical tests", *Journal of Political Economy*, 81, 607–636.

Feltham, G. and J. Ohlson (1995), "Valuation and clean surplus accounting for operating and financial activities", *Contemporary Accounting Research*, Spring, 689–731.

Financial Accounting Standards Board (1995), *Statement of Financial Accounting Standards No. 121: Accounting for the Impairment of Long-Lived Assets and for Long-Lived Assets to be Disposed Of*, Norwalk, CT.

Financial Accounting Standards Board (1998), *Statement of Financial Accounting Standards No. 133: Accounting for Derivative Instruments and Hedging Activities*, Norwalk, CT.

Florou, A. and U. Kosi (2011), *The economic consequences of mandatory IFRS adoption for debt financing.* Working paper, University of Macedonia and Lancaster University.

Florou, A. and P.F. Pope (2012), "Mandatory IFRS adoption and investor asset allocation decisions", *The Accounting Review*, forthcoming.

Foster, N. (2003), *The FASB and the capital markets. The FASB report*, Norwalk, CT, FASB, 2003.

Francis, J., R. LaFond, P. Olsson and K. Schipper (2004), "Costs of equity and earnings attributes", *The Accounting Review*, 79(4), 967–1010.

Francis, J., R. LaFond, P. Olsson and K. Schipper (2005), "The market pricing of accruals quality", *Journal of Accounting and Economics*, 39, 295–327.

Francis, J., D. Nanda and P. Olsson (2008), "Voluntary disclosure, earnings quality and cost of capital", *Journal of Accounting Research*, 46(1), 53–99.

Francis, J.R. and X. Martin (2010), "Acquisition profitability and timely loss recognition", *Journal of Accounting and Economics*, 49(1–2), 161–178.

Gebhardt, W.R., C.M.C. Lee and B. Swaminathan (2001), "Toward an implied cost of capital", *Journal of Accounting Research*, 39, 135–176.

Glosten, L. and R. Milgrom (1985), "Bid, ask and transaction prices in a specialist market with heterogeneously informed traders", *Journal of Financial Economics*, 14, 71–100.

Gode, D. and P. Mohanram (2003), "Inferring the cost of equity using the Ohlson-Juettner, Model", *Review of Accounting Studies*, 8, 399–431.

Gode, D. and P. Mohanram (2008), *Improving the Relationship between Implied Cost of Capital and Realized Returns by Removing Predictable Analysts Forecast Errors.* Working Paper, New York University and Columbia University.

Gow, I.D., G. Ormazabal and D.J. Taylor (2010), "Correcting for cross-sectional and time-series dependence in accounting research", *The Accounting Review*, 85, 483–512.

Gramming, J., D. Scjiereck and E. Theissen (2001), "Knowing me, knowing you: trader anonymity and onformed trading in parallel markets", *Journal of Financial Markets*, 4.

Greenstein, M. and H. Sami (1994), "The impact of the SEC's segment disclosure requirement on bid-ask spreads", *The Accounting Review*, January, 179–199.

Grossman, S.J. and J.E. Stiglitz (1980), "On the impossibility of informationally efficient markets", *American Economic Review*, 70, 393–408.

Guay, W. and R.E. Verrecchia (2007), *Conservative disclosure.* Working paper, University of Pennsylvania.

Hail, L. and C. Leuz (2006), "International Differences in the Cost of Equity Capital: Do Legal Institutions and Securities Regulation Matter?", *Journal of Accounting Research*, 44, 485–532.

Hail, L. and C. Leuz (2009), "Cost of capital effects and changes in growth expectations around U.S. cross-listings", *Journal of Financial Economics,* 93, 428–454.

Hamada, R.S. (1972), "The Effect of the Firm's Capital Structure on the Systematic Risk of Common Stock", *Journal of Finance*, 27, 435–452.

Handa, P. and S. Linn (1993), "Arbitrage Pricing with Estimation Risk", *Journal of Financial Economics*, 81–100.

Healy, P., A. Hutton and K. Palepu (1999), "Stock Performance and Intermediation Changes Surrounding Sustained Increases in Disclosure", *Contemporary Accounting Research*, 16, 485–520.

Hughes, J., J. Liu and J., Liu (2007), "Information, Diversification, and Cost of Capital", *The Accounting Review*, 82, 705–729.

Ibbotson and Associates (2005), *Cost of Capital 2005 Yearbook*, Chicago, Illinois.

Jagannathan, R. and Z. Wang (1996), "The Conditional CAPM and the Cross-section of Expected Returns", *Journal of Finance*, 51, 3–53.
Jegadeesh, N., and S. Titman (1993), "Returns to Buying Winners and Selling Losers: Implications for Stock Market Efficiency", *Journal of Finance*, 48, 65–91.
Johnston, J. (1984), *Econometric Methods*, McGraw-Hill, Inc., 3th Edition.
Jorgensen, B. and M. Kirschenheiter (2007), *Voluntary Disclosure of Sensitivity*. Working Paper, Columbia University.
Karamanou, I. and G. Nishiotis (2009), "Disclosure and the cost of capital: Evidence from the market's reaction to firm voluntary adoption of IAS", *Journal of Business Finance and Accounting*, 36, 793–821.
Khurana, I.K. and P. Michas (2011), "Mandatory IFRS adoption and the US home bias", *Accounting Horizons*, 25(4), 729–753.
Kim, J.-B. and H. Shi (2010), *International financial reporting standards, institutional infrastructures, and cost of equity capital around the world*. Working paper, City University of Hong Kong and Fudan University.
Kim, J.-B., J. Tsui and C.H. Yi (2011), "The voluntary adoptions of international accounting standards and loan contracting around the world", *Review of Accounting Studies*, Forthcoming.
Klein, R. and V. Bawa (1976), "The Effect of Estimation Risk on Optimal Portfolio Choice", *Journal of Financial Economics*, 3, 215–231.
Kothari, S.P. (2001), "Capital Markets Research in Accounting", *Journal of Accounting and Economics*, 31, 105–231.
Kothari, S.P. and J. Zimmerman (1995), "Price and Return Models", *Journal of Accounting and Economics*, 20, 155–192.
Kyle, A.S. (1985), "Continuous Auctions and Insider Trading", *Econometrica*, 53, 1.315–1.336.
LaFond, R. and R. Watts (2008), "The information role of conservatism", *The Accounting Review*, 83, 443–478.
Lambert, R., C. Leuz and R. Verrecchia (2007), "Accounting Information, Disclosure, and the Cost of Capital", *Journal of Accounting Research*, 45, 385–420.
Landsman, W., E. Maydew and J. Thornock (2012), "The information content of annual earnings announcements and mandatory adoption of IFRS", *Journal of Accounting and Economics*, 53(1–2), 34–54.
Lang, M. and R. Lundholm (1993), "Cross-sectional determinants of analyst rating of corporate disclosures", *Journal of Accounting Research*, Autumn, 246–271.
Lang, M. and R. Lundholm (2000), "Voluntary Disclosure and Equity Offerings: Reducing Information Uncertainty or Hyping the Stock", *Contemporary Accounting Research*, 17, 623–662.
Lara, J.M.G., B.G. Osma and F. Penalva (2009a), "Accounting conservatism and corporate governance", *Review of Accounting Studies*, 14(1), 161–201.
Lara, J.M.G., B.G. Osma and F. Penalva (2009b), "The economic determinants of conditional conservatism", *Journal of Business Finance and Accounting*, 36, 336–372.

Lara, J.M.G., B.G. Osma and F. Penalva (2011), "Conditional conservatism and cost of capital", *Review of Accounting Studies*, 16(2), 247–271.

Lettau, M. and S. Ludvigson (2001), "Resurrecting the (C)CAPM: A Cross-sectional Test When Risk Premia are Time-Varying", *Journal of Political Economy*, 109, 1238–1287.

Leuz, C. (2003), "IAS Versus U.S. GAAP: Information asymmetry-based evidence from Germany's New Market", *Journal of Accounting Research*, 41, 445–472.

Leuz, C. and R.E. Verrecchia (2000), "The economic consequences of increased disclosure", *Journal of Accounting Research*, 38, 91–124.

Lev, B. (1989), "On the usefulness of earnings and earnings research: lessons and directions from two decades of empirical research", *Journal of Accounting Research*, 27, 153–192.

Li, S. (2010), "Does mandatory adoption of International Financial Reporting Standards in the European Union reduce the cost of equity capital?", *The Accounting Review*, 85(2).

Márquez-Ramos, L. (2011), "European accounting harmonization: consequences of IFRS adoption on trade in goods and foreign direct investments", *Emerging Markets Finance and Trade*, 47(5), 42–57.

Massa, M., U. Peyer and Z. Tong (2005), *Limits of Arbitrage and Corporate Financial Policy*. Working paper, INSEAD.

McInnis, J. (2010), "Earnings smoothness, average returns, and implied equity cost of capital", *The Accounting Review*, 85, 315–341.

Miller, M.H. and F. Modigliani (1966), "Some estimates of the cost of capital to the electric utility industry, 1954–57", *American Economic Review*, 56, 333–391.

Minton, B. and C. Schrand (1999), "The impact of cash flow volatility on discretionary investment and the costs of debt and equity financing", *Journal of Financial Economics*, 54, 423–460.

Ohlson, J. (1995), "Earnings, book values and dividends in security valuation", *Contemporary Accounting Research*, 661–687.

Palea, V. (2007), "The effects of the IAS/IFRS adoption in the European Union on the financial industry", *The European Union Review*, 12(1–2).

Petersen, M.A. (2009), "Estimating standard errors in finance panel data sets: comparing approaches", *Review of Financial Studies*, Advance Access, 1–46.

Petkova, R. (2006), "Do the Fama-French proxy for innovations in predictive variables?", *Journal of Finance*, 61, 581–612.

Piotroski, J. (1999), *The impact of newly reported segment information on market expectations and stock prices.* Working paper, University of Michigan.

Pope, P. and S.J. McLeay (2011), "The European IFRS experiment: objectives, research challenges and some early evidence", *Accounting and Business Research*, 41(3), 233–266.

Rouwenhorst, K.G. (1998), "International momentum strategies", *Journal of Finance*, 53, 267–284.

Schipper, K. and R. Thompson (1983), "The impact of merger-related regulations on the shareholders of acquiring firms", *Journal of Accounting Research*, 21, 184–221.

Sellhorn, T. and S. Gornik-Tomaszewski (2006), "Implications of the 'IAS regulation' for research into the international differences in accounting systems", *Accounting in Europe*, 3(1), 187–217.

Sengupta, P. (1998), "Corporate disclosure policy and the cost of debt", *The Accounting Review*, 73, 459–474.

Shanken, J. and G. Zhou (2006), *Estimating and Testing Beta Pricing Models: Alternative Methods and Their Performance in Simulations.* Working paper, Emory University.

Shima, K.M. and E.A. Gordon (2011), "IFRS and the regulatory environment: the case of US investor allocation choice", *Journal of Accounting and Public Policy*, 30(5), 481–500.

Soderstrom, N.S. and K.J. Sun (2007), "IFRS adoption and accounting quality: a review", *European Accounting Review*, 16(4), 675–702.

Stulz, R. (1999), "Globalization, corporate finance and the cost of capital", *Journal of Applied Corporate Finance*, 12, 8–25.

Suijs, J.P.M. (2008), "On the value relevance of asymmetric financial reporting policies", *Journal of Accounting Research*, 46(5), 1297–1321.

Sunder, S. (2007), *Uniform financial reporting standards: reconsidering the top-down push.* Working paper, 7–11, Yale University.

Tweedie, D. and T. Seidenstein (2005), "Setting a global standard: the case for accounting convergence", Northwestern *Journal of International Law and Business*, 25, 589–608.

Vuolteenaho, T. (2002), "What drives firm-level stock returns?", *Journal of Finance*, 57, 233–264.

Welker, M. (1995), "Disclosure policy, information asymmetry and liquidity in equity markets", *Contemporary Accounting Research*, 801–828.

Xu, Y. and B.G. Malkiel (2003), "Investigating the behaviour of idiosyncratic volatility", *Journal of Business*, 76, 613–644.

Zellner, A. (1962), "An efficient method for estimating seemingly unrelated regressions and tests for aggregation bias", *Journal of the American Statistical Association*, 348–368.

Chapter 5

Fair Value Accounting and Financial Reporting Quality

1. Introduction

Standard setters and extensive academic literature believe that fair value accounting provides the most relevant information for financial statement users (e.g. Barth, Beaver and Landsman, 2001). Fair value accounting should ensure a higher degree of transparency of financial statements, which should lead to a higher value-relevance of accounting data and a better capability of financial markets to reflect the actual value of a firm. An extensive use of fair value accounting should increase the quantity of private information brought into public domain, thus leading to a more efficient resource allocation and capital formation.

Both the FASB and IASB have issued several standards that mandate disclosure or recognition of accounting amounts using fair values. Among the most significant are those standards that explicitly relate to financial instruments. Under both US GAAP and IAS/IFRS, fair values are in fact most frequently used for financial assets and liabilities.

The recent financial crisis has turned the spotlight on fair value accounting and has led to a major policy debate involving among others the US Congress and the European Commission as well as banking and accounting regulators around the world. Critics argue that fair value accounting has significantly contributed to the financial crisis and exacerbated its severity for financial institutions all around the world. Opponents claim that fair value is not relevant and it is potentially misleading for assets that are held for a long period and, in particular, to maturity; that prices could be distorted by market inefficiencies, investor irrationality or liquidity problems; that fair values based on models are not reliable; and that fair value accounting contributes to the pro-cyclicality of the financial system (Barth 2004, Penman 2007, Benston 2008, and Ryan 2008).

On the other extreme, proponents of the fair value accounting have argued that it merely played the role of the proverbial messenger that is now being shot (e.g. Turner, 2008; Veron, 2008). Proponents have in fact argued that fair values for assets or liabilities reflect current market conditions and hence provide timely information, thereby increasing transparency and encouraging prompt corrective actions.

A few dispute that transparency is important, but the controversy rests on whether fair value accounting is indeed helpful in providing transparency or whether it leads undesirable actions on the part of banks and firms. As a result, fair value accounting has been subject to intense debate among practitioners and academics.

The purpose of this chapter is not that of discussing the role of fair value in the recent market crises, which is still largely unexplored in empirical research. Its goal is, instead, to investigate the contribution of fair value accounting to financial reporting quality and its usefulness to investors.

Fair value accounting represents the main difference between IAS/IFRS and the European Directives, which are based on the historical cost accounting. Assessing the relevance and reliability of fair value estimates provides therefore useful insight into the role that fair value accounting plays in increasing financial reporting quality.

This chapter discusses fair value accounting with a specific focus on financial instruments for three main reasons. First of all, since both US GAAP and IAS/IFRS are most frequently used for financial assets and liability, capital market research has mainly investigated the relevance and reliability of fair value for financial instruments. Empirical research on the value relevance of fair value estimates for financial instruments is indeed quite rich. Secondly, the fair value accounting for financial instruments is under deep scrutiny for banks because of the effects it can produce on the credit cycle and real economy financing.

Finally, the IASB has already issued the new international accounting standards IFRS 9, Financial Instruments, which extends the use of fair value and should come soon into force in the European Union. Moreover, in 2011 the IASB issued IFRS 13, Fair Value Measurement, which provides a single framework for measuring fair value and comprehensive evidence on "how" to measure fair value. IFRS 13 is the result of a joint project conducted by the IASB together with the FASB, whose purpose is to harmonize US GAAP and IFRS. Fair value reliability for financial instruments therefore deserves careful analysis.

2. Fair value measurement under IFRS 13

As mentioned, in 2011 the IASB issued IFRS 13, *Fair Value Measurement*, which is the result of a joint project conducted by the IASB together with FASB.

IFRS 13 has increased the convergence between IFRS and US GAAP through the same definition of fair value as well as an alignment of measurement and disclosure requirements to FAS 157.

According to IFRS 13, fair value is the price that would be received to sell an asset in an orderly transaction between market participants at the measurement date. The definition of fair value in IFRS 13 reflects an exit price notion, that is the market price from the perspective of a market participant who holds the asset.

IFRS 13 points out that fair value must be market-based, not an entity-specific, measurement. Therefore, the firm's intention to hold an asset is completely irrelevant. For instance, the application of a blockage factor to a large position of identical financial assets is prohibited given that a decision to sell at a less advantageous price because an entire holding, rather than each instrument individually, is sold represents a factor which is specific to the firm.

If observable market transactions or market information are not directly observable, the objective of fair value measurement still remains the same, that is to estimate an exit price for the asset, and the firm shall use valuation techniques.

Valuation techniques shall be consistent with the market approach, income approach or cost approach. The market approach uses prices and other relevant information generated by market transactions involving identical or comparable assets. The income approach uses valuation techniques to convert future amounts (e.g. cash flows or income and expenses) to a single present amount. According to IFRS 13, such valuation techniques include present value techniques, option pricing models – such as the Black-Scholes-Merton formula and the binomial model – and the multi-period excess earnings method. The cost approach, instead, reflects the current replacement cost, that is the amount that would currently be required to replace the service capacity of an asset.

IFRS 13 categorizes inputs to valuation techniques into a fair value hierarchy which gives the highest priority to quoted prices (unadjusted) in active markets for identical assets (Level 1 inputs) and the lowest priority to unobservable inputs (Level 3 inputs). IFRS 13 makes similar distinctions among inputs as FAS 157.

Level 1 inputs are quoted prices (unadjusted) in active markets for identical assets that the firm can access at the measurement date. With Level 1 inputs information asymmetry between management and investors is very low. Hence, quoted prices in active markets must be used whenever available.

Level 2 inputs are inputs, other than quoted prices, that are observable – either directly or indirectly – for the asset. Level 2 inputs include quoted prices for similar assets in active markets; quoted prices for identical or similar assets in markets that are not active; inputs other than quoted prices that are observable for the asset, such as interest rates and yield curves observable at commonly quoted intervals, volatilities, prepayment speeds, loss severities, credit risks, default rates; inputs that are derived principally from or corroborated by observable market data by correlation or other means. Level 2 inputs should have great reliability as they are corroborated by observable market data. As such, IFRS 13 require maximum use of observable inputs in determining fair value.

Adjustments to Level 2 inputs that are significant to the entire measurement result in a fair value measurement categorised within Level 3. Level 3 inputs are unobservable inputs for an asset fair value measurement. Unobservable inputs are inputs for which market data are not available and, therefore, need to be developed on the basis of the best information available about the assumptions that market participants would use when pricing the asset. Level 3 inputs are subject to the highest degree of information asymmetry between preparers and users.

3. Theoretical background for fair value definition as an exit price

According to IFRS 13, fair value is an *exit value*, that is, a market price from the perspective of market participants at the measurement date.

Exit price accounting is a system of accounting which uses market selling prices to measure the firm's financial position and financial performance. It departs from conventional historical cost accounting for two main reasons. Firstly, asset values are adjusted to changes in market selling prices and such adjustments are included in income. Moreover, inflation, that is, changes in the general purchasing power of money, is taken into consideration when measuring income and capital. The income statement represents profits and losses from operations as well as the inflation-adjusted gains from holding assets. Hence, profit is measured under a "comprehensive" concept which measures the total change in the asset value.

Exit price accounting is associated mainly with the works of Raymond Chambers, Robert Sterling, and Kenneth MacNeal.

Chambers (1975) makes an important distinction between measurement and valuation. Measurement is obtaining prices objectively and independently from the measurer, i.e. the accountant, whereas valuation is concerned with expectations of future benefits that could be generated by the underlying asset. Therefore, the distinction is made between the past (historical costs), the future (valuation) and the present measurement (exit prices).

Chambers bases his proposal for exit price accounting on a notion of adaptive behaviour of a firm. He sees the firm as an adaptive entity engaged in buying and selling goods and services. The firm is governed by the decisions of its managers who represent the owners' objectives and the owners consider the firm to be an instrument by which they hope to increase their real financial wealth. The notion of adaptive behaviour implies a continual attempt of the firm to adjust to the competitive business environment for the sake of survival. The firm survives and continues operations by having the ability to go into the market place with cash to take advantage of opportunities as they arrive. The business world is dynamic and business must adapt to survive. The survival of the firm depends on the amount of cash it can command and investors are interested in personal cash receipts from their association with the firm. Therefore, all major parties are interested in cash equivalents.

The concept of adaptive behaviour sees the firm as always being ready to dispose of an asset if this action is in its best interest. For instance, the firm keeps a non-current asset only if the present value of the future net cash flow from the use of the asset is greater than the present value of the expected net cash flow from an alternative investment of the exit value of the asset. At all times, the firm must consider whether an alternative opportunity for greater returns exists for its assets if they were sold and the proceeds invested. This is an opportunity cost concept, which uses the exit price as a measurement base.

Adaptive behaviour calls therefore for knowledge of the cash and current cash equivalents of the firm's net assets. The selling price reveals the firm's ability to go into the market for the purpose of adapting itself to present conditions.

Chambers also considers the question of additivity to be a key factor in support of exit price accounting.

The main products of accounting are the balance sheet and income statement. If different measurement scales are used for the different items, they cannot logically be added together, and no practical or commercial meaning can be deduced from the aggregate. According to Chambers, the use of either historical cost for some assets, of replacement cost for others, or present value for other ones or cash do not lead to a meaningful balance sheet. Nor can a jumble of historical costs based on different dates lead to a meaningful calculation of net assets.

MacNeal (1970) claims that the historical cost accounting is based on conditions which have largely ceased to exist. Towards the end of the nineteenth century firms grew larger and many became companies with a multitude of shareholders and hired managers. In the twentieth century, firms were generally owned by numerous shareholders who relied on financial statements and the media for their information about the company they owned. As a result, accounting has become more and more important for shareholders.

MacNeal argues that conventional accounting principles based on historical cost provides potentially false and misleading financial statements that do not serve decision-oriented shareholders. Shareholders cannot learn the current values of the company assets from a balance sheet based on historical cost accounting and they are also at a disadvantage compared with insiders who have this information. The ideal solution is therefore to report all profits and losses and values as determined in competitive markets.

Sterling (1970) uses a simple model – a wheat trader in a perfect market with a stable price level – to show that exit price is better than all other accounting measurements. He defines profit as the difference between capital at two points in time exclusive of additional investments by and distributions to owners. Sterling assumes that the wheat trader wishes to maximise utility, the sources of which are consumption of goods and services and command over goods and services. The criterion to decide which valuation method is the best to determine profit is, therefore, a valuation method that yields more information than others.

To be relevant, information must be useful in the decision models of accounting report users. The decision models, in turn, enable users to decide which course of action to take among several alternatives. For the wheat trader, three decision problems are: the decision to enter and stay in the market, the decision to hold either cash or wheat and the evaluation of past decisions.

The information relevant to the above decisions is: the expected future price of wheat, the expected future price of alternatives, the present selling price of wheat, the present buying price of alternatives, the price at the last evaluation, the quantity of wheat and money at the last evaluation and the present quantities. The present selling price of wheat is, however, the only item of information that is relevant to all decisions. The others are relevant to one or more, but not to all, decisions. Even when the assumption of perfect competition and stable prices is relaxed, the exit price is still superior.

Exit price accounting involves references to real-world examples because, it is argued, every figure refers to an actual market price. Some research studies suggest that market process is relatively quite objective.

Parker (1975) focuses on the relative comparability and objectivity of exit price and historical cost carrying amounts. Objectivity is defined as a consensus among valuers, whereas comparability is defined as a consensus in measurements. Using 148 business firms, Parker shows that for measures of objectivity and comparability, exit values reveal less dispersion than carrying amounts. The major cause of the lack of objectivity of carrying amounts is the dispersion of accounting estimates on useful life and residual value. McKeown (1971) focuses on a medium-sized road construction company and concluded by statistical analysis that the methods used to determine exit prices were more objective, i.e., verifiable, than others. In another study, McKeown (1973) compares four models with methods under GAAP for their objectivity (verifiability) and concludes that the exit price model is the most objective.

Finally, exit prices and changes in exit prices are considered a good proxy for the financial risk of purchasing an asset. For example, if a firm purchases an asset and its exit value differs significantly from its entry price, then the asset is a risky proposition. This financial information indicates that the purchase of such an asset should be a long-term proposition whereby economic value is recovered by value in use. Conversely, if exit prices rise dramatically, the opportunity cost of return increases and it must be operated more efficiently.

4. Exit price versus value in use

As mentioned, according to IFRS 13 fair value is an *exit value*, that is a market price from the perspective of market participants at the measurement date. The reference to a market, rather than a transaction between parties, emphasizes the requirement that the measure be non entity-specific, which means that it shall be based on a hypothetical best market price rather than on what would actually be obtained by the firm.

As mentioned, the firm's intention to hold an asset is completely irrelevant. For instance, the application of blockage factors is explicitly prohibited by IFRS 13 on the basis that a decision to sell at a less advantageous price because an entire holding, rather than each instrument individually, is sold represents a factor which is entity-specific.

Just as fair value accounting is not a new concept, it is also not new to controversy. Several academicians and practitioners have in fact raised several issues on the fair value definition as an exit price.

Some critics claim that if certain assets are purchased with a plan of operation in mind, then that plan, those operations, indeed those people who have developed that plan must first be evaluated before alternatives about the future can be considered, and it's the accountant's task to provide the data for that evaluation. Once this evaluation is made, the firm can decide whether to continue to use the assets for the purpose they were acquired or to sell them and use their proceeds otherwise. A meaningful concept of profit is the measurement of performance in terms of what was originally intended.

Barth and Landsman (1995) have however pointed out that fair value accounting based on value-in-use is the most difficult to implement because estimating value-in-use involves incorporating firm-specific and potentially private information.

Exit price measurement requires a concept of profit where the plan is always to maximise the cash equivalent of the net assets over successive short-term periods.

Bell (1951), for instance, believes that for a company other than one which deals in the simplest trading operation, such as that examined by Sterling, "such a view of the enterprise, its objectives, and its mode of thought, would just not seem to be applicable".

Adam Smith was the first to make a distinction between value in use and value in exchange. Solomons (1966) claims that value to the firm is the relevant perspective. An asset that is held rather than sold must be worth more to its owner than its exit price, otherwise it would be sold and not selling does not directly cause its owner to suffer in economic terms after a price falls. This is especially the case of non-marketable fixed assets. Such assets are usually highly specific to a particular business and may in fact be excellent investments for the firm. Because no alternative use exists for the assets outside the business their resale value may effectively be zero. Chambers would require the firm to record a loss because of the zero resale value and according to Solomons this leads to an "absurdity and a flagrant failure to measure up to the criterion of correspondence with the economic events which are being recorded".

Weston (1970) further argues that exit price accounting provides relevant information only if the company plans to liquidate its assets. If the company plans to continue in business, the information is not relevant. It may be that in a world of perfect markets, managers must decide to liquidate at year-end. However, in the real world, it is unrealistic to assume that such a decision is faced by management on a continual basis. Moreover, critics point out that Chamber's current cash equivalent of assets is determined on the assumption of a gradual and orderly liquidation. This implies that future events must be assumed when the current cash equivalent is recorded on the balance date. Therefore, if anticipations cannot be avoided in ascertaining current cash equivalent, then the exit price model itself violates the principle of exclusion of anticipatory calculations.

Larson and Schattke (1966) also point out that the cash equivalents of individual assets sold separately and the same assets sold as a package may be quite different. For example, the specialised assets of a factory may have little resale value, but when the factory is sold together with the assets, they may command a high price. The concept of current cash equivalent, with its emphasis on separability of assets, does not recognise the possibility of selling assets as one package. As assets are combined in different sets, the current cash equivalent of the different sets may be greater or less than the sum of the assets if sold individually. Thus, Larson and Schattke conclude that current cash equivalents are themselves not additive, and exit theory does not recognise the ability of the firm to adapt in terms of combinations of assets.

Finally, Benston (2008) points out that fair value expressed as exit value is useful primarily to creditors and shareholders of companies that face likely liquidation. For stockholders of and potential investors in going concerns the relevant asset values for investment decisions are values in use, that is, the present value of the net cash flows which the assets are expected to generate within the firm. Exit values clearly are not relevant to these parties, except in those instances where the assets are to be sold soon. Ryan

(2007) highlights that market-based fair values misrepresent management intent to hold an asset. Koonce *et al.* (2011) document that investors are aware of that and, therefore, they are reluctant to embrace fair values for items not to be sold soon. By conducting multiple experiments, Koonce *et al.* (2011) investigate whether and how investors' judgement of fair value relevance for financial assets is sensitive to whether management intends to sell soon versus hold to maturity. Their results show that investors judge fair value as more relevant when the company anticipates selling the financial instrument in the near-term, as compared to holding the item to maturity.

Many academicians (e.g. Benston 2008; Whittington 2008) claim that fair value should therefore reflect the opportunities related to the investment actually available to the reporting entity, that is its value in use, and entity-specific assumptions should be made. Value in use requires including future cash flows that the entity expects to receive, discounted at a rate that reflects the firm's cost of capital. Hence, value in use includes also cash inflow or outflow expected by the entity that could not be expected by other market participants.

The above discussion highlights the fact that an asset can have two important components – value in use, which emphasises a long-term approach, and value in exchange, which concentrates on a short-term approach to valuation. They reflect two different perspectives on the purpose of financial accounting which are based on two broad schools of thought, or world views.

According to Whittington (2008), the first one – which is called the "fair value view" – is characterized by the following main features: the usefulness of the financial statements for current and prospective investors and creditors is the sole objective of financial reporting; relevance is the primary characteristic required in financial statements, whereas reliability is less important; accounting information needs ideally to reflect the future, not the past, so past transactions and events are only peripherally relevant; markets are generally sufficiently complete and efficient to provide evidence for representationally faithful measurement.

The implications of the "fair value view" are that stewardship is not a distinct objective of financial statements, although its needs may be met incidentally to others; present shareholders have no special status amongst investors as users of financial statements; past transactions and events are relevant only insofar as they can assist in predicting future cash flows; prudence is a distortion of accounting measurement, violating faithful representation; cost (entry value) is an inappropriate measurement basis because it relates to a past event (acquisition) whereas future cash flow will result from future exit, measured by fair value; fair value, defined as market selling (exit) price, as in IFRS 13, should be the measurement objective; the balance sheet is the fundamental financial statement, especially if it is fair valued; comprehensive income is an essential element of the income statement as it is consistent with changes in net assets reported in the balance sheet.

The "fair value view" emphasizes the role of financial reporting in serving investors in capital markets. It seeks accounting information that has a forward-looking content, thus impounding future cash flows from a non entity specific market perspective.

The "alternative view" is more difficult to articulate than the "fair value view" because it is drawn from a wide range of constituents of the standard-setting process who are typically commenting on particular issues from a practical perspective.

As outlined by Whittington (2008), the main features of the "alternative view" are the following: stewardship, defined as accountability to present shareholders, is a distinct objective, ranking equally with decision usefulness; present shareholders of the holding company have a special status as users of financial statements; future cash flows may be endogenous, that is feedback from shareholders (and markets) in response to accounting reports may influence management decisions; financial reporting relieves information asymmetry in an uncertain world, so reliability is an essential characteristic; past transactions and events are important both for stewardship and as inputs to the prediction of future cash flows (as indirect rather than direct measurement); the economic environment is one of imperfect and incomplete markets in which market opportunities will be entity-specific.

The implications of the "alternative view" are that the information needs of present shareholders, including stewardship requirements, must be met; past transactions and events are relevant information and, together with reliability of measurement and probability of existence, are critical requirements for the recognition of elements of accounts in order to achieve reliability; prudence can enhance reliability; cost (historic or current) can be a relevant measurement basis, for example as an input to the prediction of future cash flows, as well as for stewardship purposes; the financial statements should reflect the financial performance and position of a specific entity, and entity specific assumptions should be made when these reflect the real opportunities available to the entity; performance statements and earnings measures can be more important than balance sheets in some circumstances.

Whittington highlights that the "alternative view" also seeks to serve investors, broadly defined, but it gives priority to existing shareholders and regards stewardship as an important and distinct function of financial reporting. It also seeks accounting information that is relevant to forecasting future cash flows, but it assumes that this will often be achieved by providing information that is useful input to investors' valuation models, rather than direct valuation of future cash flows. Such information may be entity specific.

Both the IASB and FASB share the "fair value view".

Some constituencies of the standard-setting process, instead, support the "alternative view". For instance, in its July 2010 Report to G20 Leaders, the Financial Stability Board claims that

> [...] while reaffirming the framework of fair value accounting, we have agreed that the accounting standards setters should improve standards for the valuation of financial instruments based on their liquidity and investor's holding horizons.

The Basel Committee (2001) seems to share the "alternative view", too. In its banking supervision regulation, the Basel Committee allows banks which use an internal rating based approach to use an alternative method for regulatory capital calculation, called PD/LGD (Probability of Default/Loss Given Default), for equity investments – even if public – that are part of a long-term customer relationship in which returns on investment are based on regular and periodic cash flows not derived from capital gains and where there is no expectation of realising any future capital gain[2]. This implies that private equities held with a strategic intent are considered closer to subordinated credits than to equity.

A value-in–use approach uses a production-oriented entity as the relevant benchmark. Instead, exit price takes the viewpoint of a manager or an investor who has to make decisions related to the liquidity of the firm and current spending power, which means that the short-term performance of the firm is more important. Therefore, as highlighted by Barth and Landsman (1995), differences between value-in-use and exit price reflect entity specific factors, such as management skill and exploiting synergies among assets. As a result, value-in-use captures the total firm value associated with an asset and is consistent with the going concern tenet of the IASB Framework. Value-in-use should be the focus of fair value accounting, unless the objective of financial statements is to reflect information from other than a going concern perspective, e.g., that of liquidation. If this were the case, exit value should be the focus. As underlined by Barth and Landsman, fair value accounting based on value-in-use is however the most difficult to implement because estimating value-in-use involves incorporating firm-specific and potentially private information. Moreover, selectively revealing their information, managers can strategically affect gains and losses recognized under fair value accounting.

---

2 The Basel Committee, in its Working Paper on Risk Sensitive Approach for Equity Exposure in the Banking Book for IRB Banks (2001), details a definition of private equities held with strategic intent which includes the following:

(a) Direct Holdings – Holdings in securities, and other financial assets whose principal values are directly related to the value of ownership interests in a commercial endeavour, whether voting or non-voting, that convey a residual interest in the assets and income of the enterprise.

(b) Indirect Holdings and Fund Investments – Holdings in a corporation, partnership, limited liability company or other type of enterprise (including any form of special purpose vehicle) that issues ownership interests and is engaged in the business of investing in the instruments defined above.

(c) Residual Interests – Holdings in residual ownership interests of commercial enterprises that allow the enterprise to waive or defer interest or other contractual remuneration to the holder, such as perpetual preferred shares.

(d) Any security (other than convertible bonds) that ranks pari passu in liquidation with any element included in (a), (b) or (c) above.

Estimating exit value for assets and liabilities is relatively easy if they are actively traded in liquid markets. The problems become more complicated if active markets do not exist.

For assets which do not have a directly observable exit price, valuation techniques must be used to measure their fair value. Valuation techniques use Level 2 or Level 3 inputs of the IFRS 13 fair value hierarchy.

Many constituencies of the standard setting process have raised the issue that sometimes it could be very difficult, or even impossible, to measure fair value without making subjective judgements. As a result, fair value would not be reliable and, therefore, decision-useful. Furthermore, cost of gathering information and estimating fair value could not exceed benefits. The IASB has agreed that requiring fair value for some investments imposes additional costs on preparers, however "these costs are justified by improved decision-usefulness information" (IFRS 9 Exposure Draft, July 2009).

The debate on fair value measurement using valuation techniques has been ongoing for decades. In particular, critics argue that fair value based on valuation techniques is less verifiable by investors, subject to greater estimation errors by management and prone to greater managerial manipulation. These shortcomings create information asymmetry between investors and managers and can be a serious threat to the reliability of fair value. Moreover, valuation techniques introduce estimation errors and make financial reporting more volatile. (Watts 2003a; Watts 2003b; Landsman 2007; Penman 2007).

Barth (2004) points out that, in a semi-strong form of market efficiency, volatility from period-to-period in fair values and, therefore, in financial statements derives from two sources. One is the firm's activity during the period and changes in economic conditions. This volatility, called *inherent volatility*, derives from economic, not accounting forces. Inherent volatility is the volatility of the asset itself.

However, there is another source of volatility, which is called estimation error volatility. Estimation error volatility is related to the fact that accountants usually do not observe the fair value of an asset and need to estimate it. Fair values obtained by valuation techniques entail estimation errors and the resulting asset volatility is attributable not only to inherent changes in economic conditions, but also to measurement errors. As pointed out by Barth (2004), to see these sources of volatility, consider an asset to be measured at fair value. x is the fair value of the asset. The mean of x is $\overline{x}$ and the variance of x is σ_x^2. At any point time, the realization of x is drawn from a distribution. The variance of x, σ_x^2, is its inherent volatility. Usually, accountants do not observe x and need to estimate it. Hence, the amount recognized in the financial statements is $X = x + \varepsilon$, where ε is the estimation error, which has a variance of σ_ε^2. Assuming X and x are uncorrelated, ${\sigma_X}^2 = \sigma_x^2 + \sigma_\varepsilon^2$. Therefore, the volatility of the recognized amount, X, is greater than the volatility of the underlying amount, x.

Inherent volatility is the volatility of x itself, that is, σ_x^2. The higher the variance of x is, the more likely it is that next period's x will differ from this period's x. That difference creates volatility in financial statements, but it is economic volatility.

When deep and liquid markets do not exist, fair values must be estimated because future cash flows are unknown and estimation error is a natural and unavoidable product of the estimation process. For fair values obtained through estimation, estimation error volatility reflects the precision of the estimates. If the estimation error is highly volatile, recognizing in financial statements a measure of the realization of x at a particular point in time has the potential to mislead financial statement users. Inherent volatility relates to relevance, which is an information notion, whereas estimation error volatility relates to reliability.

Relevance and reliability are two fundamental characteristics of financial statement information. In financial accounting, relevance means that the information is capable of making a difference to users' decisions by helping users form predictions about the outcomes of past, present, or future events and to confirm or correct expectations. Hence, relevance is an information notion. Accountants seek to measure items that are relevant to users' economic decisions. Reliability is the extent to which the measure of the item represents what it purports to represent. Hence, reliability is a measurement notion.

An accounting amount is reliable if it is verifiable, representationally faithful, and neutral. Verifiability is the extent to which different measurers would get the same amount. This assumes, as above, that there is an underlying amount, x, which accountants need to measure. Standard-setters refer to this amount as the measurement objective. In the notation used above, one measure estimates x as $X_1 = x + \varepsilon_1$, another estimates it as $X_2 = x + \varepsilon_2$, etc., where ε_i are the realizations of ε. The variance of ε captures verifiability, an important element of reliability: the lower σ_ε^2, the greater the reliability of X.

Since volatility is expected to become greater as fair value inputs become less observable, the reliability of Level 2 and Level 3 inputs to fair value measurement is a key issue for standard setting purposes.

6. Empirical evidence on fair value relevance to investors

When assessing the quality of fair value information, a natural question to ask is whether fair value information is useful to investors. Assessing the usefulness of fair value accounting has intensified in recent years as fair values have become a pervasive component of accounting regulation. In particular, the reliability of Level 2 and Level 3 inputs to fair value measurement is a key issue for standard setting purposes.

6.1 Fair value relevance for financial assets

As the IAS/IFRS adoption in Europe is relatively recent, empirical research on the fair value relevance for European firms is scarce. On the contrary, research on fair value for US firms is quite rich as fair value accounting in the US has long been used.

Furthermore, much of the research which investigates the relevance and reliability of fair value information focuses on banks as they are largely comprised of financial assets and liabilities measured at fair value.

Barth (1994), for instance, focuses on a sample of US banks with data from 1971–1990 and finds that investment securities' fair values are incrementally associated with bank share prices after controlling for their book values. However, when examined in an annual return context, results provide mixed evidence on whether unrecognised gains and losses provide incremental explanatory power relative to other components of income. One leading candidate for ambiguous finding is that the securities' gains and losses estimates contain too much measurement error relative to the true underlying changes in their market values. Using essentially the same database, Barth *et al.* (1995) confirms the Barth (1994) findings and lends support to the measurement error explanation by showing that fair value-based measures of net income are more volatile than historical cost-based measures, but incremental volatility is not reflected in bank share prices.

Several studies show that fair value relevance varies according to the source of information. Petroni and Wahlen (1995), for instance, find that fair values of equities and Treasury securities are value-relevant, whereas fair values of municipal and corporate bonds are not, thus suggesting that fair values of securities actively traded in the market are considered as more reliable. Nelson (1996) documents that fair value of bank loans, deposits and long-term debt are not value-relevant. In contrast, Barth *et al.* (1996) find that fair values of loans are value-relevant, whereas Eccher *et al.* (1996) find the value relevance of loans only in limited settings. Finally, Venkatachalan (1996) examines the value relevance of derivative fair values and finds that such fair values are positively associated with equity market value.

All these studies come before the FAS 157, *Fair Value Measurement,* issuance in the US. Prior to FAS 157, fair value was not clearly defined as exit value, nor was the procedure for estimating fair values in the absence of active markets clearly laid-out. Therefore, studies examining the value relevance of fair value information are not necessarily based on exit prices as defined in FAS 157. Moreover, firms were not required to categorize valuation inputs into the three Levels of the fair value hierarchy.

After FAS 157, research could focus directly on the fair value relevance of the three Level inputs in the fair value hierarchy.

Several studies show that investors are aware of estimation errors and, therefore, value the three levels of the fair value hierarchy differently. Kolev (2009), for instance, shows that investors decrease the weight they place on less reliable fair-value measurements.

Using a sample of large financial institutions, he documents a significant positive association between stock prices and fair values of net assets measured using unadjusted market prices (Level 1), other observable inputs (Level 2), and unobservable inputs (Level 3). However, the coefficients on mark-to-model estimates are consistently lower than those on the mark-to-market fair values (Level 1), even though the difference is significant only for Level 3 net assets.

Goh *et al.* (2009) observe significant variation in the pricing of different levels of fair value assets, with the pricing being less for mark-to-model assets, i.e. assets with lower liquidity and greater information risk, than for mark-to-market assets. They also find that the pricing of mark-to-model assets declined over the course of 2008, consistent with increasing market concerns about illiquidity and information risk associated with these assets.

Using a sample of quarterly reports by banking firms, Song *et al.* (2010) find evidence that fair value measurements of Level 1, Level 2, and Level 3 inputs are all value-relevant. However, Level 3 assets are valued less than Level 1 and Level 2 assets. In addition, coefficients on Level 3 fair values are less than 1, which suggests that investors perceive reliability concerns for Level 3 assets. As for Kolev, the lower valuation of Level 3 assets is consistent with investors decreasing the weight they place on less reliable fair value measurements.

A typical case of potential measurement errors which stem from valuation techniques is provided by private equity valuation. Since private equities do not have directly observable exit prices, valuation techniques must be used to assess their fair value. According to IFRS 13, Level 2 inputs – such as transaction and market multiples – must have the highest priority in valuation techniques as they are corroborated by observable market data. Applying market multiples to private equity valuation implies using a set of comparable companies traded in an active market.

A certain number of studies show that the performance of private equities is relatively different from that of publicly traded companies. Quigley and Woodward (2002) and Moskowitz and Vissing-Jorgensen (2002), for instance, report lower returns for private than for public equity. Cochrane (2005) also documents an extraordinary skewness of returns since most returns are modest, but there is a long right tail of extraordinary good returns. In contrast, Liungqvist and Richardson (2003) document that private equity generates excess returns on the order of five to eight percent per year relative to the aggregate public equity market.

Kim and Ritter (1999) examine the predictive ability of market multiples for private equity valuation and test price-to-earnings, price-to-sales, enterprise value-to-sales and enterprise value-to-operating cash flow ratios, which are widely recommended by academics and commonly used by practitioners. Their findings show that ratios based on historical numbers do a relatively poor job and that relevant adjustments for differences in growth and profitability should be necessary, given the wide variation of such ratios within an industry. Along the same line, Maino and Palea (2012) find that transaction and market multiples tend to overestimate exit values. Transaction multiples are in fact cases of 'revealed preferences', i.e. they refer only to successful transactions and incorporate synergy expectations as well as other positive factors which increase transaction prices, while market multiples tend to elide the idiosyncratic component of risk. Findings also show that transaction and market multiples lead to highly volatile fair values, thus proving that market-based techniques are largely affected by the economic cycle as well as by market trends, which amplify effects and value appraisals.

Finally, Fiechter and Novotny-Farkas (2011) provide evidence that value relevance of fair value estimates varies cross-sectionally and across time. Using an international sample of banks from IAS/IFRS adopting countries, they demonstrate that fair values are generally value relevant. However, valuation coefficients vary with institutional and firm-specific factors. Optionally fair valued assets appear to experience a discount in countries with low regulatory quality. Furthermore, they show that significant exposures to subprime investments results in substantially lower value relevance for financial assets at fair value. They also find that the value relevance of fair value assets has decreased as the financial crisis worsened. Taken as a whole, their findings raise concerns about the reliability of fair values and lend some support to arguments provided by opponents to fair value accounting.

6.2 Fair value relevance for non-financial assets

Because Australian, UK and US GAAP have long permitted upward asset revaluation for non-financial assets, empirical research has examined the dimensions of value relevance of revaluations in these countries. Most studies, including Easton *et al.* (1993), Barth and Clinch (1996), Barth and Clinch (1998) and Muller and Riedl (2002), focus on tangible fixed revaluations. Such assets fall into Level 3 category in the fair value measurement hierarchy and are therefore subject to a greater amount of management discretion.

Using a sample of Australian firms with data from 1984–1990, Easton *et al.* (1993) estimate annual return regressions and find that asset revaluations of tangible long-lived assets have incremental explanatory power relative to earnings and changes in earnings. Also using a sample of Australian firms but from a later period, 1991–1995, Barth and Clinch (1998) estimate annual stock price regressions to determine if financial, tangible, and intangible asset revaluations have incremental explanatory power relative to operating earnings and equity book value less the book value of revalued assets. Consistent with US-based research, Barth and Clinch (1998) find revalued investments are incrementally priced. Contrary to the view that intangible asset revaluations are likely to be noisy and uninformative, the study finds a positive association between such revaluations and share prices. However, with the exception of mining firms, they fail to find a significantly positive association between share prices and property, plant and equipment revaluations. Their study also finds little evidence indicating that independent appraiser-based revaluations are more relevant than director-based estimates. In contrast to Barth and Clinch (1998), Muller and Riedl (2002) provide evidence that the market finds asset revaluations estimates made by external appraisers more informative than those made by internal appraisers. Muller and Riedl (2002) interpret this as evidence that the market finds asset revaluation estimates based on external appraisals to be more reliable.

One potential explanation for the difference in findings between the two studies is that the Muller and Riedl (2002) research design is more powerful that the Barth and Clinch (1998) research design. However, this conclusion must be made with caution because the Muller and Riedl (2002) sample of firms is limited to a specialised industry, investment property firms, where external appraisals are an institutional feature.

Cotter and Richardson (2002) also find that external appraisals are more reliable than those made by directors for a sample of Australian firms from 1981–1994. However, Cotter and Richardson also find that independent appraisers are more likely to be used for revaluations of land and buildings and directors are more likely for investments, plant and equipment and identifiable intangibles. This suggests that firms rely on directors' superior knowledge of asset values for assets that are more specialised and difficult for outside appraisers to value.

Aboody *et al.* (1999) examine the performance prediction and pricing implications of fixed asset revaluations for a sample of UK firms from 1983–1995. Moreover, the study finds that upward revaluations are significantly positively related to changes in future performance, measured by operating income and cash from operations. The study finds that current year revaluations are significantly positively related to annual stock returns, and current year asset revaluation balances are significantly positively related to annual stock prices. However, regarding the effects of managerial incentives to manipulate asset revaluation amounts, the study finds that relations between revaluations and future performance and prices are weaker for higher debt-to-equity ratio firms. This suggests that managerial manipulation affects the usefulness of asset revaluations made by managers of firms facing the pressure of financial distress.

7. Fair value accounting, stewardship and a dual measurement and reporting model

In general, empirical research shows that fair value relevance varies according to the source of information. Several studies document that investors are aware of estimation errors and therefore value the three Level inputs in the fair value hierarchy differently. Furthermore, evidence shows that the pricing of mark-to-market fair values declines during financial market crises, thus suggesting market concerns about illiquidity and information risk associated with fair value accounting.

Benston (2008), Whittingon (2008) and Abdel-Khalik (2011) claim that fair value alone cannot help investors to properly evaluate stewardship, that is, the careful and responsible management of funds. In fact, investors would not know how much resources the management has sacrificed to obtain that fair value.

On the other hand, historical costs do not normally provide measures of value that are useful for investment decisions. However, these numbers are useful for stewardship and control decisions made by investors and their agents, corporate officers and directors, since the numbers track the amount paid for resources and their disposition.

At the time of acquisition in an open market, fair value and historical cost are in most cases equal, but they do normally diverge in subsequent periods. Following acquisition, historical cost accounting and fair value accounting provide different information and serve different purposes.

Knowledge of expected benefits (i.e. future net cash inflows) is required for ranking and sorting out competing investment alternatives. Therefore, reporting to the owners how much the entity invested to acquire an asset is not, by itself, fully informative because it does not offer any insights about the quality of that investment. In order to assess that quality, users also need to know what this investment will bring in the future – that is, the present value.

By the same token, reporting fair value alone would not inform investors of the cost of obtaining the estimated future benefits embodied in these values. Given that fair value is measured by reference to market prices, a given asset owned by two different entities will have the same fair value at any given time, but reporting only fair value does not inform investors that one entity has, for example, paid for the same asset twice as much as the other did. In order to effectively evaluate stewardship, knowledge of what that investment is expected to bring, i.e., its fair value, is not enough. External users also need to know the cost of the investment, i.e., its historical cost.

For these two roles, some academicians have claimed that a dual measurement and reporting model should be implemented as an alternative to a pure historical cost accounting or fair value accounting model (e.g. Abdel-Khalik 2011). According to this view, historical cost and fair value are neither competitors, nor substitutes for each other and both of them should be provided. An attempt to choose either one would in fact deprive investors of access to complete and useful information.

A dual measurement and reporting model could in fact be more effective for assessing the success of an investment. As highlighted by Ronen (2008),

> [...] the comparison of expected events with past events generates information that improve the ability of investors and managers to assess the reliability of future forecasts, as well as to evaluate past performance (thus fulfilling the stewardship objective) and predict future performance (thus fulfilling the informativeness objective).

References

Abdel-Khalik, A.R. (1990), *The troubles with financial statements: the need for two sets of financial statements*, The R.J. Chambers research Lecture, The Accounting Research Foundation, University of Sydney, Australia.

Abdel-Khalik, A.R. (2011), "Fair value accounting and stewardship", *Accounting Perspectives*, 9(4), 253–269.

Aboody, D., M.E. Barth and R. Kasznik (1999), "Revaluations of fixed assets and future firm performance", *Journal of Accounting and Economics*, 26, 149–178.

Aboody, D., M.E. Barth and R. Kasznik (2006), "Do firms understate stock option-based compensation expense disclosed under FAS 123?", *Review of Accounting Studies*, 11(4), 429–461.

Baiman, S. and R. Verrecchia (1996), "The relation among capital markets, financial disclosure, production efficiency, and insider trading", *Journal of Accounting Research*, 34(1), 1–22.

Barth, M.E. and G. Clinch (1996), "International differences in accounting standards: evidence from UK, Australian, and Canadian firms", *Contemporary Accounting Research*, Spring, 135–170.

Barth, M.E. and G. Clinch (1998), "Revalued financial, tangible, and intangible assets: associations with share prices and non market-based value estimates", *Journal of Accounting Research*, 36, 199–123.

Barth, M.E. (2004), "Fair Values and Financial Statement Volatility", in Claudio Borio et al. (Eds.), *The Market Discipline Across Countries and Industries*, Cambridge, MIT Press.

Barth, M.E., W.H. Beaver and W.R. Landsman (2001), "The relevance of the value relevance literature for accounting standard-setting: Another view", *Journal of Accounting and Economics,* 31(1–3), 77–104.

Barth, M.E. (2006), "Including estimates of the future in today's financial statements", *Accounting Horizons,* 20(3), 271–285.

Bartov, E., P. Mohanram and D. Nissim (2007), "Managerial discretion and the economic determinations of the disclosed volatility parameter for valuing ESOs", *Review of Accounting Studies,* 12(1), 155–179.

Basel Committee on Banking Supervision (2001), *Risk Sensitive Approaches for Equity Exposures in the Banking Book for IRB Banks.* Working paper, Bank of International Settlements.

Bell., P. (1971), "On current replacement costs and business income", in R. Sterling (Eds.), *Asset valuation and income determination,* Houston, Scholars Book Co., 27–28.

Bens, D.A. and S.J. Monahan (2004), "Disclosure quality and the excess value of diversification", *Journal of Accounting Research,* 42(4), 691–730.

Benston, G.J. (2006), "Fair-value accounting: A cautionary tale from Enron", *Journal of Accounting and Public Policy,* 25, 465–484.

Benston, G.J. (2008), "The shortcomings of fair-value accounting described in SFAS 157", *Journal of Accounting and Public Policy,* 27, 101–114.

Biddle, G. and G. Hilary (2006), "Accounting quality and firm-level capital investment", *The Accounting Review,* 81(5), 963–982.

Bushman, R.M. and A.J. Smith (2001), "Financial Accounting information and corporate governance", *Journal of Accounting and Economics,* 32(1–3), 237–333.

Cochrane, J.H. (2005), "The Risk and Return of Venture Capital", *Journal of Financial Economics,* 75(1), 3–52.

Chambers, R.J. (1966), *Accounting, evaluation and economic behaviour,* Prentice Hall, Enlgewood Cliffs, NJ.

Chambers, R.J. (1970), "Second thoughts on continuously contemporary accounting", *Abacus,* September.

Chambers, R.J. (1975), *Accounting for inflation – method and problems,* Sydney, University of Sydney.

Chambers, R.J. (1976), "Accounting for inflation – part or whole", *Accountant's Magazine,* March.

Chambers, R.J. (1977), "Value to the business Barth", in G.W. Dean & M.C. Well (Eds.), *Current cost accounting: identifying the issues,* Lancaster, UK, International Centre for Research in Accounting.

Cotter, J. and S. Richardson (2002), "Reliability of asset revaluations: the impact of appraiser independence", *Review of Accounting Studies,* 7, 435–457.

Diamond, D.W. and R.E. Verrecchia (1991), "Disclosure, liquidity, and the cost of capital", *The Journal of Finance,* 46(4), 1325–1359.

Easton, P.D., P.H. Eddey and T.S. Harris (1993), "An investigation of revaluations of tangible long-lived asset", *Journal of Accounting Research,* 31, 1–38.

Eccher, E.A., K. Ramesh and S.R. Thiagarajan (1996), "Fair value disclosures by bank holding companies", *Journal of Accounting and Economics*, 22 (1–3), 79–117.

Edwards, E. (1975), "The state of current value accounting", *Accounting Review*, April, 240.

Enria A., L. Cappiello, F. Dierick, S. Grittini, A. Haralambous, A. Maddaloni, P.A.M. Molitor, F. Pires and P. Poloni (2004), "Fair Value Accounting and Financial Stability", *Occasional Paper No. 13*, European Central Bank.

Financial Stability Board (2010), *Report to G20 Leaders,* July.

Financial Stability Board (2011), *Report to G20 Leaders,* 4 November.

Godfrey, J., A. Hodgson, A. Tarca, J. Hamilton, S. Holmes (2010), *Accounting Theory*, 7th edition, Wiley & Son, Australia.

Goh, B., J. Ng and K. Yong (2009), *Market pricing of banks' fair value assets reported under SFAS 157 during the 2008 economic crisis.* Working paper, Singapore Management University.

Hanouna, P., A. Sarin and A. Shapiro (2001), *Value of Corporate Control: Some International Evidence.* Working paper, Marshall School of Business.

Hope, O.-K. and W.B. Thomas (2008), "Managerial empire building and firm disclosure", *Journal of Accounting Research*, 46(3), 591–626.

Horton, J. and R. Macve (2000), "'Fair value' for financial instruments: how erasing theory is leading to unworkable global accounting standards for performance reporting", *Australian Accounting Review*, 11(2), 26–39.

Kanodia, C., H. Sapra and R. Venugopalan (2004), "Should intangibles be measured: What are the economic trade-offs?", *Journal of Accounting Research*, 42(1), 89–120.

Katz, D. (2008a), "Fair-value revolution", *CFO Magazine*, September, 1.

Katz, D. (2008b), "Former FDIC chief: Fair value caused the crisis", available at <www.cfo.com> (accessed October 29, 2008).

Kim, M.J.R. Ritter (1999), "Valuing IPOs", *Journal of Financial Economics*, 53(3), 409–437.

Kolev, K. (2009), *Do investors perceive marking-to-model as marking-to-myth? Early evidence from FAS No. 157 disclosure.* Working paper, New York University.

Koonce, L., K.K. Nelson and C.M. Shakespeare (2011), "Judging the Relevance of Fair Value for Financial Instruments", *The Accounting Review*, 86 (6), 2075–2098.

IASB (2009), *IFRS 9, Financial Instruments.*

IASB (2011), *IFRS 13, Fair value measurement.*

Landsman, W.R. (2007), "Is fair value accounting information relevant and reliable? Evidence from capital market research", *Accounting and Business Research*, 37 (Special Issue), 19–30.

Larson, K. and R. Schattke (1966), "Current cash equivalent, additivity, and financial action", *Accounting Review*, October.

Laux, C. and C. Leuz (2009), "The crisis of fair value accounting: making sense of the recent debate", *Accounting, Organizations, and Society*, 34(6–7), 826–834.

Ljungqvist, A. and M. Richardson (2003), *The Cash Flow, Return and Risk Characteristics of Private Equity*. Finance Working Paper, No 03-001, New York University.

Lombardo, D. and M. Pagano (2002), "Law and equity markets: A simple model", in Renneboog, L., J. McCahery, P. Moerland, T. Raaijmakers (Eds.), *Corporate Governance Regimes: Convergence and Diversity*, Oxford University Press.

Mac Neal, K. (1970), *Truth in Accounting*, Kansas, Scholars Book co., originally published in 1939.

Maines, L.A. and J.M. Wahlen (2006), "The Nature of Accounting Information Reliability: Inferences from Archival and Experimental Research", *Accounting Horizons*, 20 (December), 399–425.

Maino, R. and V. Palea (2012), "Private Equity Fair Value Measurement: A Critical Perspective on IFRS 13", *Australian Accounting Review*, forthcoming.

McKeown, J. (1971), "An empirical test of a model proposed by Chambers", *Accounting Review*, January.

McKeown, J. (1973), "Comparative application of market and cost based accounting models", *Journal of Accounting Research*, Spring.

Moskowitz, T. and A. Vissing-Jorgensen (2002), "The returns to entrepreneurial investment: A private equity premium puzzle?", *American Economic Review*, 92, 745–778.

Muller, K.A. III and E.J. Riedl (2002), "External monitoring of property appraisal estimates and information asymmetry", *Journal of Accounting Research*, 40, 865–881.

Nelson, K. (1996), "Fair value accounting for commercial banks: An empirical analysis of FAS No. 107", *The Accounting Review*, 71(2), 161–182.

Parker (1975), "Testing comparability and objectivity of exit value accounting", *Accounting Review*, July.

Paton, W.A. and A.C. Littleton (1940), *An introduction to corporate accounting standards*, American Accounting Association, Evanston, IL.

Peasnell, K.V. (1982), "Some formal connections between economic values and yields and accounting numbers", *Journal of Business Finance and Accounting*, 9(3), 361–381.

Penman, S.H. (2007), "Financial reporting quality: is fair value plus or minus?", *Accounting and Business Research*, 37(Special Issue), 33–44.

Petroni, K. and J.M. Wahlen (1995), "Fair values of equity and debt securities and share prices of property-liability insurer", *The Journal of Risk and Insurance*, 62(4), 719–737.

Plantin, G., H. Sapra, and H.S. Shin (2008), "Fair value accounting and financial stability", *Financial Stability Review*, 12, Banque de France, Paris.

Quigley, J.M. and S.E. Woodward (2002), *Private equity before the crash: Estimation of an index*. Unpublished Working Paper, University of California at Berkeley.

Ronen, J. (2008), "To fair value or not to fair value: A broader perspective", *Abacus*, 44 (2), 181–208.

Solomons, D. (1966), Review article, *Abacus*, December, 208.
Song, C.J., W.B. Thomas and H. Yi (2010), "Value Relevance of FAS No. 157 Fair Value Hierarchy Information and the Impact of Corporate Governance Mechanisms", *The Accounting Review*, 85(4), 1375–1410.
Staubus, G.J. (2004), "Two views of accounting measurement", *Abacus*, 40(3), 265–279.
Sterling, R. (1970), *Theory of the measurement of enterprise income,* Kansas, University Press of Kansas.
Sterling, R. and K. Lemke (1982), *Maintenance of capital: financial vs. physical*, chapter 1, Kansas, Scholars Book Company.
Wallace, M. (2002), "Performance reporting under fair value accounting", *North American Actuarial Journal*, 6(1), 28–61.
Wallison, P.J. (2008), *Fair value accounting: a critique*, AEI Outlook Series, American Enterprise Institute for Public Policy Research, July.
Weston, F. (1970), "Response to evidence for a market selling price accounting system", in R. Sterling (Eds.), *Theory of the measurement of enterprise income*, Kansas, University Press of Kansas.
Whittington, G. (2008), "Fair Value and the IASB/FASB Conceptual Framework Project: a Different View", *Abacus,* 44(2), 139–168.

Conclusions

Standard setters, regulators and policy makers all have vital interest in the effect of financial reporting on the economy. This interest is due to the economic consequences associated with financial information. Financial information influences investors' behaviour with respect to portfolio selection, which affects security prices and, therefore, the terms on which a firm obtains additional financing. This, in turn, affects the firm's cost of capital and alters the nature of the projects undertaken.

In a capitalist economy, securities markets are the primary vehicle whereby capital is raised and allocated to competing investment needs. Consequently, it is socially desirable that these markets work well. From this perspective, regulators expect financial reporting to play a fundamental role in reducing information asymmetries.

Good financial reporting provides favourable climate for capital markets because of its effect on the perceived fairness of such markets. Investors are more willing to invest funds in markets if there is greater disclosure and less risk of fraud or misrepresentation about the productive opportunities of the firm issuing securities. The subsequent marketability of securities is also a function of the perceived fairness of capital markets. If capital markets are efficient with respect to a rich, comprehensive information system, investors are less concerned about information asymmetries at the time they buy and sell their securities and they are more willing to invest. On the contrary, information asymmetries negatively affect capital markets with damages for economic growth, job creation and personal wealth.

One important step in the modernization process of the accounting model in Europe is represented by Regulation 1606/2002. According to this Regulation, for each financial year starting on or after 1 January 2005, companies governed by the law of a member state must prepare their consolidated accounts in conformity with IAS/IFRS if, on their balance sheet date, their securities are admitted to trading on a regulated market of any member state. Regulation 1606/2002 also provides an option for member states to permit or require the application of international accounting standards in the preparation of annual accounts and to permit or require their application by unlisted companies.

As the explicit purpose of Regulation 1606/2012 is to ensure a high degree of transparency and comparability of financial statements, requiring IAS/IFRS for financial reporting involves that such standards are deemed both to provide a high degree of transparency in financial statements and to ensure a high degree of comparability among financial statements of firms from different countries which previously used domestic GAAP based on the European Directives. Quality and comparability of financial reporting are therefore expected to improve after the IAS/IFRS adoption.

As stated by Regulation 1606/2002, the final goal of adopting IAS/IFRS in the European Union is to ensure the effective and efficient functioning of the capital market. A higher level of transparency in financial reporting should lower the estimation risk premium which arises from information asymmetries and, therefore, the firm's cost of capital. By enhancing comparability, the IAS/IFRS adoption at the European level should also reduce cross-country differences in the cost of capital, thus fostering an equal footing competition for financial resources among firms.

Empirical research provides evidence supporting the expectation that the IAS/IFRS adoption improve financial reporting quality. However, it also shows that financial reporting quality is determined not only by the quality of accounting standards, but also by the legal and political system of the country in which firms reside as well as by financial reporting incentives.

Similarly, the mandatory IAS/IFRS adoption is not a condition *per se* to improve cross-country comparability in financial reporting. As accounting quality is a function of the overall institutional setting, research concludes that, in general, some cross-country differences in accounting quality are likely to remain even after accounting standardization through the IAS/IFRS adoption in Europe.

The link between accounting information and the firm's cost of capital is another key issue in accounting regulation. Regulation 1606/2002 states in fact that one of the expected effects of the IAS/IFRS implementation in Europe is a reduction in the firms' cost of capital.

Taken as a whole, empirical research supports the notion that adopting IAS/IFRS increases market liquidity, decreases transaction costs for investors, lowers cost of capital, and facilitates international capital formation and flows. However, research shows that also in this case effects differ according to the level of regulatory enforcement and firms' incentives. Many studies cite a wide range of other factors that can outweigh any beneficial effects of the IAS/IFRS adoption, such as extent and nature of government involvement in the economy; government involvement in financial reporting practices such as political influence of managers, corporations, labour unions, and banks; legal systems such as common law versus code law and shareholder litigation rules; securities regulation and regulatory bodies; depth of financial markets; financial market structure, such as closeness of the relationship between banks and clients; the roles of the press, financial analysts, and ratings agencies; size of the corporate sector; structure of corporate governance such as relative roles of labour, management, and capital; extent of private versus public ownership of corporations, of family-controlled businesses and of corporate membership in related company groups; extent of financial intermediation; role of small shareholders versus institutions and corporate insiders; use of financial statement information, including earnings, in management compensation; status, independence, training, and compensation of auditors. Empirical research documents in fact that such variables have led to an application of IAS/IFRS which is not uniform across Europe.

Fair value is one of the most important innovations in accounting in Europe, where financial reporting has always been based on historical cost accounting.

Fair value accounting is expected to ensure a higher degree of transparency of financial statements, to lead to a higher value-relevance of accounting data and to improve the capability of financial markets to reflect the actual value of a firm. An extensive use of fair value accounting should increase the quantity of private information brought into public domain, thus leading to a more efficient resource allocation and capital formation.

The recent financial crisis has turned the spotlight on fair value accounting and has led to a major policy debate involving among others the

US Congress and the European Commission as well as banking and accounting regulators around the world.

Critics argue that fair value accounting has significantly contributed to the financial crisis and exacerbated its severity for financial institutions all around the world. Opponents claim that fair value is not relevant and it is potentially misleading for assets that are held for a long period and, in particular, to maturity; that prices could be distorted by market inefficiencies, investor irrationality or liquidity problems; that fair values based on models are not reliable; and that fair value accounting contributes to the pro-cyclicality of the financial system. On the other extreme, proponents of the fair value accounting have argued that it merely played the role of the proverbial messenger that is now being shot. Proponents have in fact argued that fair values for assets or liabilities reflect current market conditions and hence provide timely information, thereby increasing transparency and encouraging prompt corrective actions. As a result, fair value accounting has been subject to intense debate among practitioners and academicians.

When assessing the quality of fair value information, a natural question to ask is whether fair value information is useful to investors. Assessing the usefulness of fair value accounting has intensified in recent years as fair values have become a pervasive component of accounting regulation.

In general, empirical research shows that fair value relevance varies according to the source of information. Several studies document that investors are aware of estimation errors and therefore value the three Level inputs in the fair value hierarchy differently. Investors decrease in fact the weight they place on less reliable fair-value measurements. Furthermore, evidence shows that the pricing of mark-to-market fair values declines during financial market crises, thus suggesting market concerns about illiquidity and information risk associated with fair value accounting.

Several academicians also claim that fair value alone cannot help investors to properly evaluate stewardship, that is, the careful and responsible management of funds. In fact, investors would not know how much resources the management has sacrificed to obtain that fair value. On the other hand, historical costs do not normally provide measures of value which are useful for investment decisions. Historical cost and fair value should not be considered as substitutes for one another and an attempt to choose either one would deprive investors of access to complete and useful information. For this reason, some academicians have come to the conclusion that a dual measurement and reporting model should be implemented. In this view, a dual measurement and reporting model could be more effective for assessing investment success.

Overall, this monograph shows that academic research is a valuable resource for standard setting and policy-making purposes. Financial reporting issues are often broad, difficult and complex. Academic research can however provide inputs to their resolution. It can help standard setters and regulators structure their thinking about such issues and provide evidence that inform the debate on them. From this point of view, this monograph shows that academic research can be successful in supporting the evaluation of possible effects of accounting standards and regulations.

Appendices

Appendix 1
Current use of IAS/IFRS in the countries of G20

Country	*Status for listed companies as of December 2011*
Argentina	Required for fiscal years beginning on or after 1 January 2012
Australia	Required for all private sector reporting entities and as the basis for public sector reporting since 2005
Brazil	Required for consolidated financial statements of banks and listed companies from 31 December 2010 and for individual company accounts progressively since January 2008
Canada	Required from 1 January 2011 for all listed entities and permitted for private sector entities including not-for-profit organisations
China	Substantially converged national standards
European Union	All member states of the EU are required to use IFRS as adopted by the EU for listed companies since 2005
France	Required via EU adoption and implementation process since 2005
Germany	Required via EU adoption and implementation process since 2005
India	India is converging with IFRS at a date to be confirmed.
Indonesia	Convergence process ongoing; a decision about a target date for full compliance with IFRS is expected to be made in 2012
Italy	Required via EU adoption and implementation process since 2005
Japan	Permitted from 2010 for a number of international companies; decision about mandatory adoption by 2016 expected around 2012
Mexico	Required from 2012
Republic of Korea	Required from 2011
Russia	Required from 2012
Saudi Arabia	Required for banking and insurance companies; full convergence with IFRS currently under consideration
South Africa	Required for listed entities since 2005
Turkey	Required for listed entities since 2005
United Kingdom	Required via EU adoption and implementation process since 2005
United States	Allowed for foreign issuers in the US since 2007; US SEC committed to global accounting standards and IFRS best placed to meet that need in the US, awaiting decision regarding use of IFRS for domestic companies

Source: <www.ifrs.org>, accessed January, 2013.

Appendix 2
Regulation (EC) No 1606/2002 of the European Parliament and of the Council of 19 July 2002 on the application of international accounting standards
Official Journal L 243, 11/09/2002 P. 0001–0004

THE EUROPEAN PARLIAMENT AND THE COUNCIL OF THE EUROPEAN UNION,

Having regard to the Treaty establishing the European Community, and in particular Article 95(1) thereof,
Having regard to the proposal from the Commission(1),
Having regard to the opinion of the Economic and Social Committee(2),
Acting in accordance with the procedure laid down in Article 251 of the Treaty(3),

Whereas:

(1) The Lisbon European Council of 23 and 24 March 2000 emphasised the need to accelerate completion of the internal market for financial services, set the deadline of 2005 to implement the Commission's Financial Services Action Plan and urged that steps be taken to enhance the comparability of financial statements prepared by publicly traded companies.

(2) In order to contribute to a better functioning of the internal market, publicly traded companies must be required to apply a single set of high quality international accounting standards for the preparation of their consolidated financial statements. Furthermore, it is important that the financial reporting standards applied by Community companies participating in financial markets are accepted internationally and are truly global standards. This implies an increasing convergence of accounting standards currently used internationally with the ultimate objective of achieving a single set of global accounting standards.

(3) Council Directive 78/660/EEC of 25 July 1978 on the annual accounts of certain types of companies (4), Council Directive 83/349/EEC of 13 June 1983 on consolidated accounts (5), Council Directive 86/635/EEC

of 8 December 1986 on the annual accounts and consolidated accounts of banks and other financial institutions (6) and Council Directive 91/674/EEC of 19 December 1991 on the annual accounts and consolidated accounts of insurance companies (7) are also addressed to publicly traded Community companies. The reporting requirements set out in these Directives cannot ensure the high level of transparency and comparability of financial reporting from all publicly traded Community companies which is a necessary condition for building an integrated capital market which operates effectively, smoothly and efficiently. It is therefore necessary to supplement the legal framework applicable to publicly traded companies.

(4) This Regulation aims at contributing to the efficient and cost-effective functioning of the capital market. The protection of investors and the maintenance of confidence in the financial markets is also an important aspect of the completion of the internal market in this area. This Regulation reinforces the freedom of movement of capital in the internal market and helps to enable Community companies to compete on an equal footing for financial resources available in the Community capital markets, as well as in world capital markets.

(5) It is important for the competitiveness of Community capital markets to achieve convergence of the standards used in Europe for preparing financial statements, with international accounting standards that can be used globally, for cross-border transactions or listing anywhere in the world.

(6) On 13 June 2000, the Commission published its Communication on "EU Financial Reporting Strategy: the way forward" in which it was proposed that all publicly traded Community companies prepare their consolidated financial statements in accordance with one single set of accounting standards, namely International Accounting Standards (IAS), at the latest by 2005.

(7) International Accounting Standards (IASs) are developed by the International Accounting Standards Committee (IASC), whose purpose is to develop a single set of global accounting standards. Further to the restructuring of the IASC, the new Board on 1 April 2001, as one of its first decisions, renamed the IASC as the International Accounting Standards Board (IASB) and, as far as future international accounting standards are

concerned, renamed IAS as International Financial Reporting Standards (IFRS). These standards should, wherever possible and provided that they ensure a high degree of transparency and comparability for financial reporting in the Community, be made obligatory for use by all publicly traded Community companies.

(8) The measures necessary for the implementation of this Regulation should be adopted in accordance with Council Decision 1999/468/EC of 28 June 1999 laying down the procedures for the exercise of implementing powers conferred on the Commission(8) and with due regard to the declaration made by the Commission in the European Parliament on 5 February 2002 concerning the implementation of financial services legislation.

(9) To adopt an international accounting standard for application in the Community, it is necessary firstly that it meets the basic requirement of the aforementioned Council Directives, that is to say that its application results in a true and fair view of the financial position and performance of an enterprise – this principle being considered in the light of the said Council Directives without implying a strict conformity with each and every provision of those Directives; secondly that, in accordance with the conclusions of the Council of 17 July 2000, it is conducive to the European public good and lastly that it meets basic criteria as to the quality of information required for financial statements to be useful to users.

(10) An accounting technical committee should provide support and expertise to the Commission in the assessment of international accounting standards.

(11) The endorsement mechanism should act expeditiously on proposed international accounting standards and also be a means to deliberate, reflect and exchange information on international accounting standards among the main parties concerned, in particular national accounting standard setters, supervisors in the fields of securities, banking and insurance, central banks including the ECB, the accounting profession and users and preparers of accounts. The mechanism should be a means to foster common understanding of adopted international accounting standards in the Community.

(12) In accordance with the principle of proportionality, the measures provided for in this Regulation, in requiring that a single set of international

accounting standards be applied to publicly traded companies, are necessary to achieve the objective of contributing to the efficient and cost-effective functioning of Community capital markets and thereby to the completion of the internal market.

(13) In accordance with the same principle, it is necessary, as regards annual accounts, to leave to Member States the option to permit or require publicly traded companies to prepare them in conformity with international accounting standards adopted in accordance with the procedure laid down in this Regulation. Member States may decide as well to extend this permission or this requirement to other companies as regards the preparation of their consolidated accounts and/or their annual accounts.

(14) In order to facilitate an exchange of views and to allow Member States to coordinate their positions, the Commission should periodically inform the accounting regulatory committee about active projects, discussion papers, point outlines and exposure drafts issued by the IASB and about the consequential technical work of the accounting technical committee. It is also important that the accounting regulatory committee is informed at an early stage if the Commission intends not to propose to adopt an international accounting standard.

(15) In its deliberations on and in elaborating positions to be taken on documents and papers issued by the IASB in the process of developing international accounting standards (IFRS and SIC-IFRIC), the Commission should take into account the importance of avoiding competitive disadvantages for European companies operating in the global marketplace, and, to the maximum possible extent, the views expressed by the delegations in the Accounting Regulatory Committee. The Commission will be represented in constituent bodies of the IASB.

(16) A proper and rigorous enforcement regime is key to underpinning investors' confidence in financial markets. Member States, by virtue of Article 10 of the Treaty, are required to take appropriate measures to ensure compliance with international accounting standards. The Commission intends to liaise with Member States, notably through the Committee of European Securities Regulators (CESR), to develop a common approach to enforcement.

(17) Further, it is necessary to allow Member States to defer the application of certain provisions until 2007 for those companies publicly traded both in the Community and on a regulated third-country market which are already applying another set of internationally accepted standards as the primary basis for their consolidated accounts as well as for companies which have only publicly traded debt securities. It is nonetheless crucial that by 2007 at the latest a single set of global international accounting standards, the IAS, apply to all Community companies publicly traded on a Community regulated market.

(18) In order to allow Member States and companies to carry out the necessary adaptations to make the application of international accounting standards possible, it is necessary to apply certain provisions only in 2005. Appropriate provisions should be put in place for the first-time application of IAS by companies as a result of the entry into force of the present regulation. Such provisions should be drawn up at international level in order to ensure international recognition of the solutions adopted,

HAVE ADOPTED THIS REGULATION:

Article 1
Aim
This Regulation has as its objective the adoption and use of international accounting standards in the Community with a view to harmonising the financial information presented by the companies referred to in Article 4 in order to ensure a high degree of transparency and comparability of financial statements and hence an efficient functioning of the Community capital market and of the Internal Market.

Article 2
Definitions
For the purpose of this Regulation, "international accounting standards" shall mean International Accounting Standards (IAS), International Financial Reporting Standards (IFRS) and related Interpretations (SIC-IFRIC interpretations), subsequent amendments to those standards and related interpretations, future standards and related interpretations issued or adopted by the International Accounting Standards Board (IASB).

Article 3

Adoption and use of international accounting standards

1. In accordance with the procedure laid down in Article 6(2), the Commission shall decide on the applicability within the Community of international accounting standards.

2. The international accounting standards can only be adopted if:

– they are not contrary to the principle set out in Article 2(3) of Directive 78/660/EEC and in Article 16(3) of Directive 83/349/EEC and are conducive to the European public good and,

– they meet the criteria of understandability, relevance, reliability and comparability required of the financial information needed for making economic decisions and assessing the stewardship of management.

3. At the latest by 31 December 2002, the Commission shall, in accordance with the procedure laid down in Article 6(2), decide on the applicability within the Community of the international accounting standards in existence upon entry into force of this Regulation.

4. Adopted international accounting standards shall be published in full in each of the official languages of the Community, as a Commission Regulation, in the Official Journal of the European Communities.

Article 4

Consolidated accounts of publicly traded companies

For each financial year starting on or after 1 January 2005, companies governed by the law of a Member State shall prepare their consolidated accounts in conformity with the international accounting standards adopted in accordance with the procedure laid down in Article 6(2) if, at their balance sheet date, their securities are admitted to trading on a regulated market of any Member State within the meaning of Article 1(13) of Council Directive 93/22/EEC of 10 May 1993 on investment services in the securities field(9).

Article 5

Options in respect of annual accounts and of non publicly-traded companies

Member States may permit or require:

(a) the companies referred to in Article 4 to prepare their annual accounts,

(b) companies other than those referred to in Article 4 to prepare their consolidated accounts and/or their annual accounts, in conformity with the international accounting standards adopted in accordance with the procedure laid down in Article 6(2).

Article 6

Committee procedure

1. The Commission shall be assisted by an accounting regulatory committee hereinafter referred to as "the Committee".

2. Where reference is made to this paragraph, Articles 5 and 7 of Decision 1999/468/EC shall apply, having regard to the provisions of Article 8 thereof. The period laid down in Article 5(6) of Decision 1999/468/EC shall be set at three months.

3. The Committee shall adopt its rules of procedure.

Article 7

Reporting and coordination

1. The Commission shall liaise on a regular basis with the Committee about the status of active IASB projects and any related documents issued by the IASB in order to coordinate positions and to facilitate discussions concerning the adoption of standards that might result from these projects and documents.

2. The Commission shall duly report to the Committee in a timely manner if it intends not to propose the adoption of a standard.

Article 8

Notification

Where Member States take measures by virtue of Article 5, they shall immediately communicate these to the Commission and to other Member States.

Article 9

Transitional provisions

By way of derogation from Article 4, Member States may provide that the requirements of Article 4 shall only apply for each financial year starting on or after January 2007 to those companies:

(a) whose debt securities only are admitted on a regulated market of any Member State within the meaning of Article 1(13) of Directive 93/22/EEC; or

(b) whose securities are admitted to public trading in a non-member State and which, for that purpose, have been using internationally accepted standards since a financial year that started prior to the publication of this Regulation in the Official Journal of the European Communities.

Article 10

Information and review

The Commission shall review the operation of this Regulation and report thereon to the European Parliament and to the Council by 1 July 2007 at the latest.

Article 11

Entry into force

This Regulation shall enter into force on the third day following that of its publication in the Official Journal of the European Communities.

This Regulation shall be binding in its entirety and directly applicable in all Member States.

Done at Brussels, 19 July 2002.

For the European Parliament

The President

P. Cox

For the Council

The President

T. Pedersen

(1) OJ C 154 E, 29.5.2001, p. 285.

(2) OJ C 260, 17.9.2001, p. 86.

(3) Opinion of the European Parliament of 12 March 2002 (not yet published in the Official Journal) and Decision of the Council of 7 June 2002.

(4) OJ L 222, 14.8.1978, p. 11. Directive as last amended by European Parliament and Council Directive 2001/65/EC (OJ L 283, 27.10.2001, p. 28).

(5) OJ L 193, 18.7.1983, p. 1. Directive as last amended by European Parliament and Council Directive 2001/65/EC.

(6) OJ L 372, 31.12.1986, p. 1. Directive as last amended by European Parliament and Council Directive 2001/65/EC.

(7) OJ L 374, 31.12.1991, p. 7.

(8) OJ L 184, 17.7.1999, p. 23.

(9) OJ L 141, 11.6.1993, p. 27. Directive as last amended by European Parliament and Council Directive 2000/64/EC (OJ L 290, 17.11.2000, p. 27).

Appendix 3

Implementation of the IAS Regulation (1606/2002) in the EU and EEA **(published for information purposes only)** **Date: 07/02/2012** **page: 1**

European Commission	Austria	Belgium	Bulgaria	Cyprus	Czech Rep.	Denmark
Status of the implementation of IAS/IFRS	Final law	Final law	Final law	Final law	Final law	Final law
Article 5(a) of the IAS Regulation LISTED COMPANIES **1.** Does your MS use the option to **permit** IAS in the **annual accounts** for listed companies?	No	No	No	No	No	Fin. entities: Yes Other entities: Yes, for annual accounts for listed companies which do prepare consolidated accounts.
2. Does your MS use the option to **require** IAS in the **annual accounts** for listed companies?	No	Yes, for real estate investment companies (SICAFI/BEVAK)	Yes	Yes	Yes	Fin. entities: No Other entities: Yes for annual accounts for listed companies which do not prepare consolidated accounts.
Article 5(b) of the IAS Regulation OTHER COMPANIES **1.** Does your MS use the option to **permit** IAS in the **consolidated accounts** for other companies? If yes, what type of companies?	Yes, all companies	Yes, all companies	Yes, for SMEs[1]	No	Yes All types of companies	Yes, all types
2. Does your MS use the option to **require** IAS in the **consolidated accounts** for other companies? If yes, what type of companies?	No	Yes, for credit institutions, and investment firms	Yes, for all other types of companies, except SMEs and entities in liquidation and insolvency	Yes, all companies	No	No
3. Does your MS use the option to **permit** IAS in the **annual accounts** for other companies? If yes, what type of companies?	No	No	Yes, for SMEs	No	No	Yes, all types
4. Does your MS use the option to **require** IAS in the **annual accounts** for other companies? If yes, what type of companies?	No	No	Yes, for all other types of companies, except SMEs and entities in liquidation and insolvency	Yes, all companies	No	No
Article 9 of the IAS Regulation **(a)** Did your MS use the option to **defer** the application of IAS **until 2007** for companies whose debt securities only were admitted on a regulated market of any MS?	Yes	Yes	No	No	No	Fin. entities: No Other entities: Yes
(b) Did your MS use the option to **defer** the application of IAS **until 2007** for companies whose securities were admitted to public trading in a non-member State and which, for that purpose, had been using internationally accepted standards since a financial year that started prior to the publication of the IAS Regulation in the OJ?	Yes	Yes	No	No	No	No
Miscellaneous Was earlier adoption (before 2005) of IAS allowed? If yes, for what type of companies/ from when?	Yes, consolidated accounts since 1998	Yes, cons. accounts for all companies	a) Yes, mandatory for listed companies, banks, insurance and investment undertakings from 1.01.2003 b) Other companies - voluntary application from 01.01.2003	Yes (a) Requirement of the Institute of Certified Public Accountants of Cyprus for all companies since 1981 (b) Requirement of the Stock Exchange legislation for listed companies since 2003	Yes all types of companies	Yes for 2004. The annual and consolidated accounts for all companies except for financial companies.

1 Bulgarian SMEs must use the same accounting framework (IAS or national GAAP) for both annual and consolidated accounts.

European Commission	**Estonia**	**Finland**	**France**	**Germany**	**Greece**	**Hungary**	**Ireland**
Status of the implementation of IAS/IFRS	Final law	Final law	Final law	Final law	Final law	Final law	Final law
Article 5(a) of the IAS Regulation **LISTED COMPANIES** **1.** Does your MS use the option to **permit** IAS in the **annual accounts** for listed companies?	No	Yes[2]	No	No, but additionally to still required local GAAP	No	No, but additionally to still required local GAAP	Yes
2. Does your MS use the option to **require** IAS in the **annual accounts** for listed companies?	Yes	No	No	No	Yes	No	No
Article 5(b) of the IAS Regulation **OTHER COMPANIES** **1.** Does your MS use the option to **permit** IAS in the **consolidated accounts** for other companies? If yes, what type of companies?	Yes All types other than below	Yes[3], all types	Yes	Yes, all types	Yes, some companies[3]	Yes, all types of companies within the scope of Accounting Act	Yes, all types
2. Does your MS use the option to **require** IAS in the **consolidated accounts** for other companies? If yes, what type of companies?	Yes. Credit institutions, insurance undertakings, financial holding companies, mixed financial holding companies, investment firms	No	No	Yes, companies, which have filed for a listing	Yes, banks, and other financial institutions	No	No
3. Does your MS use the option to **permit** IAS in the **annual accounts** for other companies? If yes, what type of companies?	Yes, all types other than below	Yes[2,3]	No	No, but additionally to still required local GAAP	Yes, some companies[3]	No, but additionally to still required local GAAP	Yes, all bar companies not trading for gain
4. Does your MS use the option to **require** IAS in the **annual accounts** for other companies? If yes, what type of companies?	Yes. Credit institutions, insurance undertakings, financial holding companies, mixed financial holding companies, investment firms	No	No	No	Yes, banks, and other financial institutions	No	No
Article 9 of the IAS Regulation **(a)** Did your MS use the option to **defer** the application of IAS **until 2007** for companies whose debt securities only were admitted on a regulated market of any MS?	No	Yes	Yes	Yes	No	Yes	Yes
(b) Did your MS use the option to **defer** the application of IAS **until 2007** for companies whose securities were admitted to public trading in a non-member State and which, for that purpose, had been using internationally accepted standards since a financial year that started prior to the publication of the IAS Regulation in the OJ?	No	No	N/A	Yes	No	No	No
Miscellaneous Was earlier adoption (before 2005) of IAS allowed? If yes, for what type of companies/ from when?	Yes All types 01.01.2003	1. Listed companies consolidated accounts 30.9.2003 2. Other companies (not insurance companies): all accounts 2004	No	Yes, cons. acc. option for listed companies (as from 1998) and for unlisted comps from 2003	31.12.2004 Yes, some companies[3]	No, but additionally to still required local GAAP	No

2 Finland: Not insurance companies.

3 Finland and Greece: Companies, which are audited by certified auditors.

European Commission	**Italy**	**Latvia**	**Lithuania**	**Luxemburg**	**Malta**	**Netherlands**
Status of the implementation of IAS/IFRS	Final law	Final law	Final law	Final law[4] Law proposal	Final law	Final law
Article 5(a) of the IAS Regulation **LISTED COMPANIES** **1.** Does your MS use the option to **permit** IAS in the **annual accounts** for listed companies?	No, even for insurance companies	No	No	Yes	No	Yes
2. Does your MS use the option to **require** IAS in the **annual accounts** for listed companies?	Yes[5], except for insurance companies	Yes	Yes	No	Yes	No
Article 5(b) of the IAS Regulation **OTHER COMPANIES** **1.** Does your MS use the option to **permit** IAS in the **consolidated accounts** for other companies? If yes, what type of companies?	Yes, except for small enterprises and required companies	Yes, all types (except for banks, insurance commercial companies and other supervised financial institutions)	Yes, all types, except banks and other credit institutions, insurance companies	Yes, all types	Yes, all other than those listed below	Yes, all types
2. Does your MS use the option to **require** IAS in the **consolidated accounts** for other companies? If yes, what type of companies?	Yes, for some companies[6]	Yes, banks, insurance commercial companies and other supervised financial institutions	Yes, for banks and other credit institutions	No	Yes, for banks, insurance companies, certain other supervised financial institutions and larger companies deemed significant in the local economy	No
3. Does your MS use the option to **permit** IAS in the **annual accounts** for other companies? If yes, what type of companies?	Yes, except for insurance, small enterprises and required companies	No	Yes, all types, except banks and other credit institutions, insurance companies	Yes, all types	Yes, all other than those listed below	Yes, all types
4. Does your MS use the option to **require** IAS in the **annual accounts** for other companies? If yes, what type of companies?	Yes, some companies[7]	Yes, banks, insurance commercial companies and other supervised financial institutions	Yes, for banks and other credit institutions	No	Yes, for banks, insurance companies, certain other supervised financial institutions and larger companies deemed significant in the local economy	No
Article 9 of the IAS Regulation **(a)** Did your MS use the option to **defer** the application of IAS **until 2007** for companies whose debt securities only were admitted on a regulated market of any MS?	No	No	No	Yes	No	No
(b) Did your MS use the option to **defer** the application of IAS **until 2007** for companies whose securities were admitted to public trading in a non-member State and which, for that purpose, had been using internationally accepted standards since a financial year that started prior to the publication of the IAS Regulation in the OJ?	No	No	No	Yes	No	No
Miscellaneous Was earlier adoption (before 2005) of IAS allowed? If yes, for what type of companies/ from when?	No	Yes, banks, insurance companies, other supervised financial institutions had to use IAS before 2005	Yes, for banks and other credit institutions since 1997	Derogations on an individual basis	Yes all types of companies	No

4 Luxembourg: final law for banks and insurance companies; law proposal for common law companies.

5 Italy: Listed insurance enterprises must comply with IASs only if they do not draw up consolidated accounts.

6 Italy: Supervised financial companies; companies with financial instruments widely distributed among the public; insurance companies.

7 Italy: Supervised financial companies; companies with financial instruments widely distributed among the public.

European Commission	Poland	Portugal	Romania	Slovakia
Status of the implementation of IAS/IFRS	Final law	Final Law	Final law	Final law
Article 5(a) of the IAS Regulation **LISTED COMPANIES** **1.** Does your MS use the option to **permit** IAS in the **annual accounts** for listed companies?	Yes	Yes	No, but for purposes of information only. Annual financial statements that are in line with the Accounting Regulations conform to the Fourth Directive are required in the relation with the Government authorities.	Yes, if not companies of public interest[8]
2. Does your MS use the option to **require** IAS in the **annual accounts** for listed companies?	No	Yes if the statutory accounts are the only accounts that they published to the market. Also credit institutions, other financial institutions and insurance undertakings applying local GAAP (which is consistent with IAS/IFRS), have to provide additional disclosures on the changes and impacts that would result from applying IAS/IFRS.	Yes, for credit institutions	Yes, companies of public interest[8]
Article 5(b) of the IAS Regulation **OTHER COMPANIES** **1.** Does your MS use the option to **permit** IAS in the **consolidated accounts** for other companies? If yes, what type of companies?	Yes, 1) companies having filed for admission to public trading; 2) any parent comp. being a subsidiary of another parent undertaking preparing its consolidated accounts in line with IAS	Yes, all types	Yes. According to the Order of the minister of public finance no. 3055/2009 in force, the entities applying the Accounting Regulations conform to the European Directives, excepting the credit institutions and the entities whose securities are admitted to trading on a regulated market, and which have the obligation to draw up consolidated financial statements, may apply in this regard either IFRS or Accounting Regulations conform to the Seventh Directive.	No
2. Does your MS use the option to **require** IAS in the **consolidated accounts** for other companies? If yes, what type of companies?	Yes, banks	Yes, for credit institutions and other financial institutions in 2006	Yes, for credit institutions.	Yes, any type of companies
3. Does your MS use the option to **permit** IAS in the **annual accounts** for other companies? If yes, what type of companies?	Yes, 1) companies having filed for admission to public trading; 2) companies whose parent undertaking prepares its consolidated accounts in line with IAS	Yes, companies within the scope of consolidation of an entity who applies IAS/IFRS and also insurance undertakings not within a scope of consolidation. Credit institutions and other financial institutions are excluded	No, but for purposes of information only. Financial statements that are in line with the Accounting Regulations conform to the Fourth Directive are required in the relation with the Government authorities.	Yes, for those listed companies and merchants with securities except banks, which are not those of public interest[8]
4. Does your MS use the option to **require** IAS in the **annual accounts** for other companies? If yes, what type of companies?	No	No	Yes, for credit institutions	Yes, for all companies of public interest[8]
Article 9 of the IAS Regulation **(a)** Did your MS use the option to **defer** the application of IAS **until 2007** for companies whose debt securities only were admitted on a regulated market of any MS?	Yes	No	Yes (starting with the financial statements for 2007 financial year)	No
(b) Did your MS use the option to **defer** the application of IAS **until 2007** for companies whose securities were admitted to public trading in a non-member State and which, for that purpose, had been using internationally accepted standards since a financial year that started prior to the publication of the IAS Regulation in the OJ?	No	No	Yes (starting with the financial statements for 2007 financial year)	No
Miscellaneous Was earlier adoption (before 2005) of IAS allowed? If yes, for what type of companies/ from when?	No	Derogations on an individual basis	Yes (starting with the financial statements for 2001 financial year), but for purposes of information only.	No

8 Companies of public interest mean the banks, Export- Import Bank of Slovak Republic, insurance companies excepting health insurance companies, stock exchange, Office of Slovak Assurors, Slovak Railroads, reinsurance companies, asset management companies and the companies, that at least in two consecutive reporting years fulfil at least two from following three preconditions: gross amount of asset over 5 billions of Slovak Crowns (approximately 149.000.000,– EUR), net turnover over 5 billions of Slovak Crowns and average number of employees over 2000.

European Commission	**Slovenia**	**Spain**	**Sweden**	**UK**
Status of the implementation of IAS/IFRS	Final Law	Final law	Final law	Final law
Article 5(a) of the IAS Regulation **LISTED COMPANIES** **1.** Does your MS use the option to **permit** IAS in the **annual accounts** for listed companies?	Yes	No	No	Yes
2. Does your MS use the option to **require** IAS in the **annual accounts** for listed companies?	No	No	No	No
Article 5(b) of the IAS Regulation **OTHER COMPANIES** **1.** Does your MS use the option to **permit** IAS in the **consolidated accounts** for other companies? If yes, what type of companies?	Yes, for companies, other than banks and insurance companies, if so decided by the assembly of the company, but for the minimum period of 5 years	Yes, all types	Yes, all types	Yes, all types of companies except for the charity sector
2. Does your MS use the option to **require** IAS in the **consolidated accounts** for other companies? If yes, what type of companies?	Yes, for banks and insurance companies	Yes, for groups in which there is a listed company.	No	No
3. Does your MS use the option to **permit** IAS in the **annual accounts** for other companies? If yes, what type of companies?	Yes, for companies, other than banks and insurance companies, if so decided by the assembly of the company, but for the minimum period of 5 years	No	No	Yes, all types of companies except for the charity sector
4. Does your MS use the option to **require** IAS in the **annual accounts** for other companies? If yes, what type of companies?	Yes, for banks and insurance companies	No	No	No
Article 9 of the IAS Regulation **(a)** Did your MS use the option to **defer** the application of IAS **until 2007** for companies whose debt securities only were admitted on a regulated market of any MS?	Yes	Yes, except for banking sector companies	Yes	No
(b) Did your MS use the option to **defer** the application of IAS **until 2007** for companies whose securities were admitted to public trading in a non-member State and which, for that purpose, had been using internationally accepted standards since a financial year that started prior to the publication of the IAS Regulation in the OJ?	No	No	No	No
Miscellaneous Was earlier adoption (before 2005) of IAS allowed? If yes, for what type of companies/ from when?	No	No	No	No

European Commission	Iceland	Liechtenstein	Norway
Status of the implementation of IAS/IFRS	Final law	Final law	Final law
Article 5(a) of the IAS Regulation **LISTED COMPANIES** **1.** Does your MS use the option to **permit** IAS in the **annual accounts** for listed companies?	Yes, for the years 2005 and 2006	Yes	Yes
2. Does your MS use the option to **require** IAS in the **annual accounts** for listed companies?	Yes, from 2007	No	No. Required for listed companies that do not prepare consolidated accounts from the financial year starting after 1. January 2011.
Article 5(b) of the IAS Regulation **OTHER COMPANIES** **1.** Does your MS use the option to **permit** IAS in the **consolidated accounts** for other companies? If yes, what type of companies?	Yes, for medium sized and big companies	Yes, all types	Yes, all types
2. Does your MS use the option to **require** IAS in the **consolidated accounts** for other companies? If yes, what type of companies?	No	No	No
3. Does your MS use the option to **permit** IAS in the **annual accounts** for other companies? If yes, what type of companies?	Yes, for medium sized and big companies from 2005	Yes, all types	Yes, all types
4. Does your MS use the option to **require** IAS in the **annual accounts** for other companies? If yes, what type of companies?	No. If the consolidated groups are permitted to use IAS in their consolidated accounts(according to question 1 in 5(b)), the annual accounts of each subsidiary are required to use IAS from 2007	No	No
Article 9 of the IAS Regulation **(a)** Did your MS use the option to **defer** the application of IAS **until 2007** for companies whose debt securities only were admitted on a regulated market of any MS?	Yes	No	Yes
(b) Did your MS use the option to **defer** the application of IAS **until 2007** for companies whose securities were admitted to public trading in a non-member State and which, for that purpose, had been using internationally accepted standards since a financial year that started prior to the publication of the IAS Regulation in the OJ?	Yes	No	Yes
Miscellaneous Was earlier adoption (before 2005) of IAS allowed? If yes, for what type of companies/ from when?	No	31.12.2002 Yes, all types	No